GLASS HOUSES

GLASS HOUSES

Saving Feminist Anti-Violence Agencies from Self-Destruction

Rebekkah Adams

Fernwood Publishing • Halifax & Winnipeg

Editing: Brenda Conroy
Printed and bound in Canada by Hignell Book Printing

Published in Canada by Fernwood Publishing
Site 2A, Box 5, 32 Oceanvista Lane
Black Point, Nova Scotia, B0J 1B0
and #8 - 222 Osborne St., Winnipeg, Manitoba, R3L 1Z3
www.fernwoodpublishing.ca

Fernwood Publishing Company Limited gratefully acknowledges the financial support
of the Government of Canada through the Book Publishing Industry Development
Program (BPDIP), the Canada Council for the Arts and the Nova Scotia
Department of Tourism and Culture for our publishing program.

Library and Archives Canada Cataloguing in Publication

Adams, Rebekkah
Glass houses: saving feminist anti-violence agencies from self-destruction
/ Rebekkah Adams.

Includes bibliographical references.
ISBN 978-1-55266-265-6

1. Abused women--Services for--Canada. 2. Women's shelters--
Canada. I. Title.

HV1448.C3A43 2008   362.88082'0971   C2007-907022-1

CONTENTS

This is for my mother, Patricia Wilson (Alexander).
You made me everything. This world is darker without you.

ACKNOWLEDGEMENTS

My deepest respect to the women who embrace violence against women work and who changed my life — so many on my journey; however, the women of YBH, Tricia, Anna and Jo, will always have a special place. The community of women once blossoming at TWC have my lifelong admiration. Special gratitude to Linda for being her and endless respect to Bonita who has partnered Nemesis.

Gratitude and love to my sister Cindy and to my lifelong friend and soul mate Lisa.

To my husband Troy and my two sons Aidan and Calder, with whom I have discovered a depth of love I could not have imagined, eternal thanks.

PREFACE

When my mother was beaten, she fled most often to the bathroom, which was the only room in the house with a door that locked; it afforded her some meagre sense of safety. While there, she would wash the blood off. Other times, she fled to her bedroom, opened her Bible and looked for solace. But she never left the house. There was simply nowhere to go.

Then in the early 1970s, even prior to 1974 and the opening of Interval House in Toronto, my mother attended a secret meeting above a store in downtown Toronto. It wasn't put on by an organization, nor did it have a structure or even a clear leader. I believe my mother found an ad in the newspaper — a tiny clipping — and plotted some way of attending. It changed my mother forever. A small group of women sat together in that borrowed space and talked. That was it. Talked about how they were beaten by their husbands. Talked about how it felt. Spoke about the shame and their belief that it had only been happening to them.

This was an awakening for my mother in two ways. First, she had found a connection in relation to her experience. The women in that group were all given the gift of insight into the scope of wife beating. It wasn't just them after all. They knew this grotesque phenomenon went far beyond that group of women to who knows how many others. Second, my mother was given the gift of humility. She admitted to me that as a grown woman she expected that the group of women would be comprised of a certain "type" of woman, that they would be of a lower "class" somehow and that she in her middle-class pain was simply an aberration. She discovered that one woman was married to a doctor; one was a professor at the University of Toronto. These women crossed all class boundaries.

The importance of this secret meeting goes beyond the lessons it provided for my mother. This was the germination of women creating space in which to heal from violence. This meeting had been organically grown from one woman's pain when she invited others with similar pain simply to talk. Women were joining together out of commonality, without the endorsement of any government-funded agency, without a "trained" group facilitator, without an agenda or short-term goal-focused planning. It was the birth of a community of "battered" women.

Interval House opened in 1974, and my mother and I were two of the first residents. From a child's perspective it appeared to be utter pandemonium

— families of different cultures whirling about the kitchen and a housesitter, as she was known, ladling out chicken noodle soup. And that was it. There were bunk beds to sleep in and a bathroom to share, and a roof over our heads and the lock on the door of the house no one knew existed, and the relief that he could not get us in there.

The years 1972 to 1982 were a decade prior to "legitimizing" services, and then came the 1982 to 1984 guilt-fuelled implosion of money into shelters after the members of the House of Commons had originally broken out laughing about the issue. After this implosion of money, the next requirement was that of staff qualifications and then came the separation between women and those that helped them. It became the professional helping the victim, or client. In 1995 cuts came to the funding, and the notion of making space for each other was gone. Staff worried about job protection, about themselves, about giving way....

I entered the shelter system, the anti-violence movement, as a child consumer in tow with my mother, who thanked God there was finally somewhere to go to escape the horrific abuses of my father. In those fledgling years, there was no programming as we have defined it now and certainly no resources or supports for the children of violence. There were playrooms in basements or back rooms filled with donated toys with missing pieces and some glue and scissors and maybe a bean bag, but no one to talk to, no-one who understood.

I re-entered the same shelter years later as a young teenager, wanting to give something to other kids who were residents there, but after a try at volunteering with no direction and no internal supports, I abandoned the idea.

Eighteen and in first-year university, I saw an advertisement in the paper for a Relief Children's Advocate Worker, and I was entranced. I wrote the most passionate cover letter of my life, detailing my understanding to date of violence against women and kids and my experience with shelters. I attached a resume with only camp counselling and restaurant experience. Miraculously, not only was I granted an interview, I managed to secure the position, and so began the journey.

I worked relief positions in several shelters throughout university, thinking that soon I'd figure out what I wanted to do with my life and would get a real job. It took years to sink in that this was actually a real job and that I couldn't divorce myself from this work even though I tried to run off and become a journalist. Anti-violence work drew me back, not so much as a moth to a flame, but a seeker to the Mecca, the wanderer back home.

There is something about this work that cannot be found in any other place in the world — a community of strength, wisdom and passion. The very best of women.

Gradually as I moved through organizations and roles, life changes and learnings, I saw that I was always hungry for answers as to why such ideals of peace and equity were often places of inequality and pain. I adopted a personal need to review in this context how we get to the places we get to.

I witnessed hierarchies that set apart clients and management in the most grotesque of classist distancing, where an executive director and her managers abused power in the same way I had experienced in the "outside" world of men. I witnessed members of collectives eating women up in their misuse of power despite the absence of actual structural power, finding it by recreating unhealthy family dynamics, silencing other members with shame and assuming false victimization.

Perhaps most heartbreaking of all, I witnessed the most egalitarian, community-based, healthy and peaceful group of women I had ever come to know be destroyed by an agency that was devoid of feminist leadership, was drunk on fear and dysfunction and which accused this group of women of running a "cult."

I wondered if anything had really improved since the days women simply gathered together at unmarked locations and opened their hearts. I felt we had lost most of the drive and innocence that united the women who spearheaded the movement, who initially risked their lives to use these services. I wondered where the sense of community had gone.

INTRODUCTION

Today's political climate is precarious for women's services, especially those that are clearly feminist-based. Current governments, notwithstanding party politics, strongly favour gender-neutral services, which appear to be moving toward a health-care catch-all of counselling regarding violence against women and children. Agencies that have been woefully underfunded and shamefully ignored for years still do not receive enough government money to operate, relying on fundraising to sustain the most basic of services. Instead of restoring funding cuts made a decade and more ago and topping up funding to humane levels, our government is providing monies for fundraising training. The media is quick to zone in on mismanaged anti-violence organizations, and ministries are eager to support audits of these services whether they are warranted or not. Women's services are pitted against one another to compete for funding that is far too meagre for the need.

The writing is on the wall. Funding will be cut unless women and men raise their voices to ensure that the issue of violence against women is not lost amid an agenda of policing and health, returning woman abuse back to the dark ages of the pre-1980s. Anti-violence organizations need to be structured to withstand this war upon them by a public and government that find truth distasteful. We need to be ready to transform outmoded and unworkable models and bring in a new organizational structure that can serve as a healthy container for this unique work. We need to create agencies that are sustainable and healthy and models for other workplaces. We need to become workplace coaches to show mainstream organizations the strengths of feminist organizational theory and how they can adapt it for themselves. We must become role models for organizational health and practice. We need to put into practice what we know and preach, instead of destroying ourselves and our own organizations. There are plenty of enemies who relish watching us fail. Many of them even work among us.

Recently I have been drawn to workshops and presentations on healthy workplaces and related topics and have discovered that there has been a shift in thinking regarding the creation of organizational health. I was dismayed however to realize that instead of being at the forefront of such ideas, women's organizations are sadly lagging behind the mainstream. Why have feminist organizations not addressed these issues and why are we not the model of organizational health?

INTRODUCTION

This book offers a glimpse into the problem areas of feminist organizations and creative suggestions from women working within this field. It contains the voices and experiences of women who have vast collective experience, voices and ideas that are too often suppressed and discounted. At the very least, perhaps these ideas can spark further brainstorming on how to facilitate effective change to maintain our essential services before they are lost. We must not have a hand in their undoing.

Much of the research for this book has been accomplished during twenty years of work in women's shelters and sexual assault centres, both collectives and hierarchies. During the last seven years in particular, I surveyed women within many anti-violence organizations: women's shelters, rape crisis centres, community-based outreach services — services that self-identified as feminist and those that did not. In those anti-violence agencies that did not identify as feminist, I found that the majority of the individual staff did and that the choice of the agency to identify as non-feminist was most often a decision by a board of directors that felt that it was a more accurate representation of its community.

In conducting my research, I found some resistance, often not where I anticipated it. Those who did resist this work did so mostly out of fear that it might be used to further marginalize the gains women in the anti-violence sector have made. I understand and wholly appreciate this fear. However, I have witnessed the destruction from within of several organizations and have found myself at a place of spiritual emptiness. What I have come to is the need to be true to the feminist commitment to self-analysis and critical thinking about systems and structures, even if that means our own. This book is a starting point for dialogue and self-examination, the beginning of an open discourse that can lead to promoting organizational health.

I feel that many of us in the anti-violence sector are committed to feminist theory and its application in a way that simply applies rhetoric. We are not continuing our own critical analysis. Such complacency is dangerous and is too often felt and carried alone by women of colour and lesbians within our organizations. It will eventually spell our own demise. In not actively examining our own work as anti-violence advocates, we, and I mean in particular we as white women, are permitting that cosy comfortable place of white privilege to once again give us a nice quiet place to snuggle up in. As Laura Brown states, "We must build an ethical imperative of self-confrontation of racism as a first step…. This first step makes all others possible because it allows us, without shame or guilt, to attend to reality so as to change" (1991: 124).

After examining the material I had gathered and read and re-read, several themes emerged. These provided me with a structure by which to group ideas and concepts, although I still struggled with the order that should be given to these themes. The general intent is not to say that all or any of these themes apply to any given organization at any one time, but that many are present at various stages of organizational growth, moving with fluidity as changes move through the internal climate.

This book is not intended as a history lesson about the feminist movement or the shelter or rape crisis centre movement, or as any sort of comparative study of male/female led organizations. I began with the assumption that the reader will be at least familiar with anti-violence work, anti-violence organizations, feminist organizations, feminist theory or women's workplace studies.

This book is not intended to be a rant about any specific organization; themes emerging reflect those common to anti-violence workplaces. I do think that many observations can also be applied to other workplaces, but there are certain unique characteristics of agencies that deal with violence against women and children that have helped to create unique problems. I have included some quotes from women who participated in my research, identified only by initials, as a compromise for those who were fearful of identification.

Many valuable resources already exist that organizations can draw from to create workplace health. Many of my findings mirror what is highlighted elsewhere, and what I hope can be achieved is a continued dialogue within and among agencies to promote sustainable organizations. Such existing materials and new ideas birthed from this book will ideally serve to stir debate and introspection.

CHAPTER 1

ORGANIZATIONAL STRUCTURE

INTRODUCTION

The political, social and cultural context of an anti-violence agency or environment affects the staff. The very nature of the work is political and linked to the values of society. The feminist philosophy of an individual juxtaposed against the organizational structure can create personal conflicts. Racism and homophobia can create a bias in how the service is provided and in the relationships between co-workers. The philosophical underpinnings of women-centred shelters and counselling services suggest that staff and boards have moved beyond intolerance to a place of good natured solidarity. Individuals are affected more deeply when the intolerance comes from within (Richardson 2001: 18).

Attempting to structure any "human services" work environment immediately causes one to run into a conceptual roadblock, as noted in Janet Finn's article "Burnout in the Human Services: A Feminist Perspective." Professional training professes the importance of autonomy and self-regulation, and workers are disillusioned to find that these concepts have no place in a bureaucracy. "Ironically, social workers struggle to promote the empowerment and self-determination of clients — the very values that are antithetical to the structure in which they are employed" (Finn 1990: 62).

Creating a field of work that serves victims of violence is in and of itself a contradiction. We imposed a vision of "work" on a "profession" that was constructed within a male workforce, according to a male career framework. We imposed this patriarchal framework upon a belief system whose driving premise was that patriarchy was bad, damaging and not serving the needs of women. The fallout for women of living within this patriarchal society demonstrated itself as violence, oppression, and resistance to change. This is what women were fighting. The shelter movement emerged from the women's liberation movement, and now that we were getting serious about creating safety for battered women, we fell back into using the same old patriarchal ways of constructing institutions, and ended up divorcing ourselves from the roots of change. We ignored the social uprising of women in order to allow our agencies and organizations to be created. Maybe we were in a hurry and saw a window of opportunity to develop anti-violence and women-run organizations, and perhaps we never had the time, background, experience or skills to develop new, more appropriate frameworks for the radical thinking that drove the need.

I think in living with this contradiction from the very beginnings of women-run anti-violence organizations, we have felt a sense of this construct as wrong, as if we were wearing the wrong size shoes, and many of the current insidious destructive dynamics have grown out of this sense that the idea and the method are diametrically opposed. What this has created is a type of organizational cancer, not immediately visible, but attacking our core and making us weak from the inside.

Placing this lens over some of the destructive behaviours that have been seen in such agencies explains some of the incredulous feelings that have been experienced by wounded staff. For example, a woman who had been with one particular shelter for years, since its inception, and who was vital to the community's awareness of woman abuse, found herself accused of oppressing some co-workers. She found that the manner in which these "victimized" women displayed their displeasure was abusive, that they used tactics she felt were representative of the abusers they all profiled in the course of their work. What made it harder for this woman to think through her possible role in the purported oppression was the fact that her agency was implementing, continuing and supporting a system of internal workplace operation that had grown more and more mainstream and increasingly bureaucratic, and that mirrored the very male-based systems the agency fought against — the ones women found to be oppressive.

The nature of anti-violence work is fundamentally isolating and changes the perspective from which one sees and operates within the world. Those who have chosen this as a career find themselves reframing their experience of safety within their own community and families, re-thinking relationships, their worldview altered and intellectual virginity raped. Janet Finn argues that "providers of human services experience the isolation, alienation, devaluation, and powerlessness felt by their clients and... this experience is the natural outgrowth of work environments in which feminist values are discounted." She proposes that "the articulation and operationalization of the feminist values of interdependence and mutual support through processes of empowerment in the workplace are necessary conditions for addressing burnout. These values must be personalized and politicized to create more responsive, proactive service delivery systems" (1990: 56).

As soon as we transferred violence-against-women advocacy, protection, resistance and education into "work" and paid work, we created the patriarchal framework that accompanied it. We created the need for rules and policy and legislation and contracts and collective agreements and funding agreements. We created an environment we labelled "accountability" but that had little or nothing to do with the issues we were fighting and everything to do with forcing women into yet another structure fraught with power and control issues. The patriarchal model of paid work allowed women to focus on violence-against-women work without being compromised by providing uncompensated service but enslaved women into job descriptions and hierarchies and the potential for re-victimization within a "power over" dynamic. This is a dynamic in which order is maintained by virtue of a fear-based structure, where women could be fired, disciplined, grieved, sanctioned and supervised. This re-creation of power levels churned through years of employment relationships with many casualties.

It created an environment where even sister services — shelters and sexual assault centres — vied with each other to ascertain which was the more "hard done by" and the most trauma-based service. The "work" itself became and compartmentalized. We competed for recognition and compensation based on who was the greater victim within the service provision framework, who had the most stress in their jobs, who worked with the neediest victims, who needed more education to obtain the job.

With society ready to shut us down, financially and politically, we are now seeing the dark ages coming again, a regression in societal commitment to changing violence against women. This is evident in the push for gender-neutral services. Without a plan, resources and organization, we will be destroyed.

There are simply not enough women in power. Therefore, there are no models and no one to emulate or take heed of. Those women who have stepped into the male political ring and have any degree of power, however token, are simply not using their influence to back our issues, but instead merely try to fit into the boys' clubs. Women who are permitted voices and space within the media and popular culture are often those who bash their own gender and work counter-productively to our cause.

Women are not backing women. There is a split between "feminists" and "other women." There is too often a sense of superiority and disdain on the part of each "side," directed at the other "side." Not embracing our sisters, regardless of our framework, is part of the making of our undoing. We need their help. We need a common ground to unite us. Janet Finn states our perilous situation beautifully:

> The feminist movement grew out of the personal and political de-valuation of women and points to women's need to control not only their lives, but their access to power and resources. The broad goal of feminism being individual liberation through collective activity embracing both personal and social change. This goal is predicated on the values of interdependence, mutual support, and equity. Feminism requires an appreciation of process and an understanding context.

A feminist approach to human services emphasizes empowerment, participatory decision making and acknowledgement of the inter-dependent worker-client environment. It demands a commitment to the removal of oppressive barriers through politicizing the personal and personalizing the political. (1990: 61)

Finn states that "we need to move toward a developmental process in the workplace that is based not on the inevitability of exhaustion but on the potential for growth." The appreciation for diversity would be encouraged within a context of commonality. And according to Finn, "Collective action would be promoted for personal and institutional change" (1990: 67).

All domination takes the form of administration.
— Herbert Marcuse

As we professionalized anti-violence work, we created jobs, we created careers, and many women who had never been members of the "workforce" had paying jobs assisting other women, many of whom had come from similar experiences. In the giving over of the volunteer, socially conscious woman to the paid professional, we opened ourselves up to all kinds of restrictions of speech and social and political action. Now that we were funded by govern-ment money, we faced challenges around legitimacy and accreditation, but also the piggish economic machine that assigned worth to work, the good old patriarchal system of our modern economic structure.

The work of women, the real unpaid, unrecognized work of bearing and raising children, maintaining household and family, health care in the home and countless other overlooked functions has never been counted by the system of modern economics. Thus, it has no value. It does not gener-ate any money. Since women are not seen as contributing to the economic health of society, we are not counted and are, in fact, obsolete in the eyes of the financial systems that run the world, like the International Monetary Fund, the World Bank, the United Nations Economic Fund.

Marilyn Warring eloquently links these concepts together in her ground-breaking film *If Women Counted*. Amazingly, of all the women I interviewed during the course of my research, only a handful had even heard of this film. When they saw it, they were validated. So many of the basic concepts underlying the gender dynamics that feed the violence we seek to end are rooted here. Yet when many of these women wanted to show the film to others within their organizations, they were refused. Most disturbingly, they were refused by the administrators within their agencies — board, executive directors and senior managers. Women are not a visible population, and when you are invisible, you are not visible when policy is made and wealth and benefits are distributed. Therefore, women view themselves as the subculture, rather than the culture, despite the larger number of women and the core societal reproductive function we carry out.

Once we legitimized our work by generating a paycheque off the backs of women's pain, we were put in the duplicitous position of requiring our own victimization in order to guarantee our personal financial security. No victims, no job. But at least now we weren't helping out of the goodness of our hearts, we weren't volunteering. We had paid work and a workplace comprised solely of other women, which seemed friendly and safe within the world of male-dominated workplaces and the injustices and harassments we had received there.

Now that we had established our superiority over unpaid women in this field, we were faced with the task of justifying our role in the mental health-dominated world of "helping." People in this field were "professionals" with degrees and titles and legitimacy. This was thrown in our faces in many ways, but most glaringly in the justice system as we accompanied women to fight for their rights in family court. Depending on the jurisdiction, this hasn't changed all that much within the court system, but within the not-for-profit community our status has risen. We now have titles and benchmark work or life experience that enable us to be hired within many agencies. Many of us are "over qualified" for our job description and definitely for the pay scale.

Now not only are we benefiting from victimization, we are feeling "professional" about it — retaining a smug superiority over the unpaid, untrained grandmothers of this work. We use our skills and qualifications to lobby for increases in pay, respect, titles and promotions. We have allowed ourselves to become part of the hierarchy of the worth of women who work versus women who don't.

It is in the economy's best interests to keep the violence continuing, as there is no value in peace. It is in our best interests to have the violence continue, so we can lobby for pay raises and better benefits. If the violence against our own gender were eradicated, we would be unemployed, many of us unskilled outside our specific field, and forced into poverty with no secure future. The nature of our work is counterproductive to our own personal security. This must have an impact on how we perceive our roles in anti-violence work. Consciously or not, this must feed our experience. Yet we never talk about it.

And, in fact, the structures we create to benefit "victims" are rarely examined to ensure we are working towards true emancipation from violence. The same old rhetoric is there, in newsletters and fundraising campaigns, but we do not examine our programs and structures through a lens of freedom for women. In order to be truly ethical we must talk about the implications of anti-violence work as paid work. We must discuss poverty, work, money, control and other related issues frequently and examine our programs with a critical lens.

Why are we talking about poverty? This is a violence-against-women agency.
— an executive director

STRATEGIC PLANNING AND MISSION STATEMENT

So much energy, so many resources and so much rhetoric go into the myriad strategic plans created and occasionally implemented by anti-violence organizations. There are rarely any concrete beneficial results from these. The structure is always the same, the plans created by consultants using mainstream models to collect data. Janet Finn challenges us to throw out the old models:

> Our institutional structures value adaptation over change. Workers and clients alike can benefit from joining together to challenge this expectation of adaptation. The application of feminist principles to planning and organizing may lead to the development of creative conflict strategies that promote the empowerment of individuals and changes in the system. Brainstorming among workers and clients would surely produce a more extensive and creative list. (1990: 67)

It is essential to have feminist boards and feminist executive directors, not simply bureaucrats in those roles. We need to create new models and processes for gathering information and transforming that information into useable plans.

It is imperative that regular reviews of mission statements are done to ensure that what you are doing as an agency is what you say you are doing and that all of what you do and how you do it is in accordance with your mission statement. Feminist anti-violence agencies tend to flounder when the global problem of violence against women is internalized by our individual agencies. We talk about violence against women as being a social or political problem, but what we do is totally individual and our responses are totally individual. Our mandates speak to things we don't actually carry out in practice. We have nice language, but we are not carrying out a feminist framework in how we operate; we are not working at changing power dynamics. We focus on individuals, perform little in the way of social action, and there is no reflection of changing power structures internally within the organizations. Our organizational values, beliefs and principles do not match *our practice*. This split, this incongruence, trips us up. The cultural commonality is collapsed because although we provide excellent services, the societal problem of violence is either steady or increasing, so pride in what we do well is run over by spiritual deflation.

As the organization or agency providing the anti-violence services evolves into a structured entity, it takes on the face of the patriarchal, the father: the rule-based, structure-based, financial accountability-driven face of the work. The female governance and management takes on the mother duplicity, of confidante and comrade, as well as authoritarian and disciplinarian. The union of mother and father, the institution of the agency as an entity unto itself, then evolves to the status of god; the uncommunicative larger intangible entity.

Within management team structures I have seen this dynamic played out: the executive director in the role of mother, managers vying for her attention and favouritism as would a group of sisters, trying to ascertain their status, their intrinsic value, while denigrating or tattling on the others. It is in this dynamic that I have witnessed the competition behind closed doors and sidebar conversations to establish who is the most overworked, the most faithful, the most knowledgeable. In meetings, I have watched issues habitually become personalized in order to gain sympathy; issues brought to the meeting table that served only to attempt to shame another manager or to get her into trouble with "mom."

BUSINESS PLAN AND STAFF MEETINGS

The very framework of most anti-violence services and the prevention program offshoots of this framework are derived from a crisis response and a recognition of need. Yet the services are not responsive to this need. If they were, they would evolve. Shelters cling desperately to their under-funded envelopes and are unwilling to examine new models that might address actual need more suitably. Such anti-violence organizations need to create business plans that will reduce the need for their own existence and they need to brainstorm much more broad and lasting solutions to the violence. We need a business plan in order to reduce the damage. We need a business plan in order to reduce the client base, not increase it. We as women and as survivors of violence have never felt believed, so we have collected statistics and numbers and occupancy rates. We have increased our client bases and our waiting lists to justify the need for our services and to garner the recognition that the violence, the problem, is there. This must stop. We can always create a demonstrable need for our services. It takes great courage to dissolve what we have evolved.

Women's organizations tend not to petition the community, and they appear to be doing a poor job of appropriate needs assessments. Since the community has the moral ownership of the agency, it needs to be consulted on service needs and direction, and often.

We are too scared to have an exchange of ideas. Staff meetings exchange information but not ideas. We are resistant to looking at new models. Ideas for new models need to derive from a woman's community. Women's organizations should be incubators of change and should offer space, inspiration and resources in which to discuss plans for something greater.

In my research one of the common themes I saw was the reluctance to have all-staff meetings. This reluctance was primarily on the part of the executive director, who often resisted the idea entirely, and when staff lobbied enough to gain one, she created an agenda full of benign information in a presentation-only format, with no room for true discussion or dialogue.

Within organizations that were failing or trying to heal from a wounded agency culture or traumatic event such as the death of a client, this was the number one request from staff in order to facilitate healing and communication. Very infrequently was this accommodated. Executive directors and senior managers fear being "blasted" by staff, and this fear leads them to continue to prevent such forums. This fear only goes underground and gets played out in more destructive, passive-aggressive ways. One of the best lessons I learned from the women I worked with when assuming the role of a new manager was to sit in on the anger and frustration and bitterness and allow them a safe, confidential, repercussion-free container in which to vent. It was amazing what I learned.

BOARDS OF DIRECTORS

First and foremost, in order to govern an organization that is by philosophy feminist, it is incomprehensible that the board would be comprised of anyone else except feminists. And women. Here is where the initial point of divergence within the anti-violence movement often begins and where it fundamentally begins to destroy itself. Many organizations have men on their boards of directors and in fact solicit and encourage male membership within the organization. Some agencies have had male executive directors, male human resources managers and male staff. We need to draw on a lesson from IBM. In order to make the company work, every individual within the company shares a vision. Every person at IBM — including the line people — is a marketer first. Within anti-violence agencies, we must be social activists first. This means everyone, from chair of the board to relief worker.

Similar to the transgender argument about what is "female" — is it physicality or lived experience — we in anti-violence organizations must have an understanding of the legacy of property, gender and class relations, and a deeper understanding of power in all its forms. The board must actively work on understanding types of power and, in doing its own deep work within, must model how relationships will be within the organization.

The board of directors is responsible for ensuring that the foundation documents and the policies of the organization accurately reflect the purpose, priorities and principles of the corporation. The agency's commitment to anti-racism and anti-oppression should be reflected in all these documents (Ontario Association of Interval and Transition Houses 2000: 10).

Many women working in this field are oblivious to the non-profit board requirement — the appointment and function of their board of directors. Accountability to the community finds its function in making the directors of the agency, the CEO and the board members representative of the community in which the organization is based. That community (collectively as taxpayers who are funding the service) has the job of holding the board accountable to ensure the agency is run according to its mandate, aims and principles.

Perhaps the most important thing here is that as women's organizations developed over the last twenty-five years, from grassroots movements to funded non-profits with charitable numbers and by-laws, a parallel evolution was occurring in the study of boards of directors and types of governance models. Because non-profit status is contingent upon having a board of directors, women's organizations and board governance grew up simultaneously, one learning from the other. The difference was that women's non-profits had no clear history or guidance from which to draw. Therefore, with the evolution of board dynamics and the struggles with governance identity and adherence to models in the nature of a captain running the ship, the *boss* of the agency, the trickle-down effect from an unclear or uncertain or worse, dysfunctional, board seeped into the culture of the agency. No one really thought to question how the board contributed to the effectiveness of the agency. Many boards were seen as a distinctly separate group that was not intrinsically connected to the life cycle of the organization.

Often, boards themselves did not have the framework to draw on in order to realize the organic way in which they should be transforming to fit their model of governance in with the different stages of the organization's life cycle. Chances are these boards didn't understand the model they were supposed to operate within. Well-meaning community members put in their time, burned out and often came away with bitterness on their tongue, and the themes within the agency's and board's makeup reoccurred.

The reality for boards changed over the years, much as the realities changed for the agencies they governed. Both came to the current point of needing to be more accountable and outcome-oriented. There is pressure for the complement of board members to reflect many things: the diversity of the community, the voice of the community, a "valued' skill base with a higher standard of experience and background. It isn't enough to be a well-meaning, interested person, and this increase in expectation has decreased the pool of community volunteers from which to draw. Agencies are competing against one another for board members, struggling to keep their numbers up and to find ways to solicit members and keep them happy. While this may be easier in urban centres, the reality in smaller and rural communities is that often the same individuals serve on multiple agency boards and are voted in term after term, allowing no new blood to flow in and risking the maintenance of a dysfunction, as well as a smattering of nepotism. The pressure on boards increases with the lack of adequate funding and the cutthroat competition for donations from the community.

While these realities exist, the goal is to structure a dynamic board that can mould itself to enhance the stage of the organizational life cycle in which the agency finds itself. A board that has been the founding board for an agency and has been instrumental in birthing the organization will clearly have a different conceptualization of its role than a board of an agency that has been operational for ten years. Where many boards and agencies get stuck is in being able to transform and change from an old model and way of working in order to enhance the agency's ability to move forward into a new developmental phase.

Vision Management, a consulting company that offers training for board development and governance models, sees the organizational life cycle as beginning with birth (foundation building), moving to development (focus on mission, vision and values), then to the growth stage (strategic alliances and partnerships) and to the fourth level, transformation (innovation). The governance model chosen must therefore be the ideal complement to the agency stage.

Board members must ensure they have an historical context into which to put their role on the board. Board policy must mandate that all board members be as informed and educated on any issue as front-line workers or internal volunteers. Board members must have a conceptualization of the political history of the women's movement and the anti-violence movement.

In most organizations volunteers who staff help lines, perform parent relief duties, drive clients to groups, answer the telephones or fold the laundry have all received some basic orientation and training in the field. The extent or intensity of the training varies, but volunteers are normally all provided with and, most importantly, expected to have an orientation or training and to go through screening. Some organizations require a probationary period and provide ongoing supervision and support in some form.

The exception is often the board of directors, the group of volunteers with the most structural power and influence. This group displays the largest lack of training, information, expertise and accountability. The urgent need for board members often decreases scrutiny, and individuals are permitted to sit on boards simply to fill the vacant seat. This must never be allowed.

Recruitment unfortunately involves getting one's friends on the board, creating a board sub-group, which can be very dangerous. When this takes priority over seeking members with specific skill sets or background, it creates a culture of nepotism without regard for quality.

With the necessity to simply fill seats becoming the priority, so come also a corresponding organizational movement to allow men onto the boards of women's organizations. So occurred a de-emphasis on any training or expectation of feminist theoretical understanding. In general we have begun to see apathy towards the critical board function of political and social action.

Through internal board-driven processes such as strategic planning, these training issues are often brought forward by front-line staff who are exasperated with witnessing how an uneducated board can derail an agency. Since the training need is identified by staff, it is often shelved or ranked lower in overall agency priority, as there exists no fundamental understanding that this *is* the agenda and it *must* drive all other aspects of the strategic plan and operation of the agency. Since staff members have brought the training gap forward, there is the structural question as to who should then offer the training, and offers from staff to train internally are often blocked. Staff at this junction can be accused of breaching structural protocol.

The necessity to ensure board members are well trained, well educated and informed falls into a structural gap. Who is accountable for ensuring that this is happening? The answer is both the community, who the board is structurally representative of, and the funding ministries. However, the funding bodies and government representatives do not often involve themselves in this aspect of program overview. The executive director or the collective are in the perilous position of holding their "bosses" accountable. Many are reluctant to proceed out of fear for their positions, as they directly answer to the board. Boards need guidance, strong internal leadership and to have training built in as an expectation of the funders, the ministry and the membership of the organization.

Board training must encompass the spectrum of feminist, anti-violence theory, board governance models and ongoing board development. The executive director and internal staff must be seen as the experts in the field of violence against women. Systems by which this knowledge can flow must be created. The board must be expected to create policies that speak to these requirements — clear policies on board training and board governance. The policies must be enforced.

Recruiting board members is not simply about filling vacant seats and maintaining the adequate number of members to comply with your by-laws. Board members need to be passionate about what they are governing and must continue to develop their understanding of the issues while they sit on the board. When advertising for board positions, it is imperative that the expectations are made clear for interested parties, not only in the context of time commitment and expectations, boundaries and such, but of a commitment to social justice action. The board needs to spearhead social justice coalitions locally and join other networks on a broader scale. It must create opportunities to involve staff in such functions, with which to break from their day-to-day work.

It should be incumbent upon board members on any board to take steps toward self improvement and board self-inventory. There are many resources within the mainstream community that can provide guidelines, frameworks, tip sheets and assessment tools with which to do this. In gaining access to these resources, the issue should not be money, and the availability should have no barriers. Many boards already have this type of information in dusty binders. The problem is that boards often do not use these tools, offer no training to new board members, do not prioritize their own work as a board and do not include it in their yearly plan, should they even be organized enough to create one.

Front-line staff members in different agencies have varying degrees of information about the board itself or its governance model, processes and functions. Many have no idea who even sits on their board. They may have seen a memo circulating but there is no mechanism to familiarize staff with board, either as individuals or with regard to roles and responsibilities. More frighteningly, executive directors often are also not familiar with governance and process, and offer no guidance or leadership to this group of community volunteers in matters of board function, limitations, governance and the internal/external relationship.

The creation and maintenance of a functioning board need not be rocket science. There are exhaustive lists of things a board can do to commit to being healthy and productive. However, most boards appear lost, without boundaries and unable to maintain healthy functioning. In this state, they lose many members and have great difficulty attracting new members. Many women interviewed said their board meetings often ran for five or six hours at a time, agendas were not adhered to and individual personality clashes often overtook the work. Boards were rife with relationships of nepotism, often with staff, and governance models were never appropriately maintained.

Of the board members I interviewed:

- no one spoke of board apprenticeship;
- no board appeared to commit time solely to concentrating on the agency's vision;
- there was a great deal of blurring between board members and non-governance work functions within the agency; and
- conflicts of interest were numerous.

And the most divisive elements were of a personal, human nature, and included the following:

- a lack of support of the board's decisions as a unified voice were reported;
- egos and personalities overtook the agenda and the work at hand;
- ethics and values were compromised;
- board members were burning out not only from not knowing their own limits, but also from inefficient meetings and functions;
- there was idle gossip, questionable confidentiality and bad faith comments and actions; and
- in some agencies there were allegations of open and covert racism and homophobia — even misogyny.

If this is the body designed to lead the agency, how healthy can it be internally? What role can boards with these issues have in governance and modelling?

What Boards Need to Do

It is crucial that the board undertakes an annual (if not more frequent during times of crisis) (1) critical self-examination of its own vision, actions and level of efficiency; (2) self-evaluation of individual members; (3) review of conflicts within the board; and (4) confirmation that the board is a reflection of the community it is designed to represent. Within a feminist anti-violence organization, this review must be reflective of feminist values and principles and must include a plan for ongoing education as a direct result of such self-examination. The board must always view its work, voice, make-up and functions through not only an anti-violence lens, but through anti-racist, anti-homophobic and anti-classist lenses as well. Such an inventory of self-reflection is easily done internally by a committed feminist board. To begin, a board may want to hire a consultant, a cost that is necessary and needs to be prioritized when establishing budgets.

The format of such self-reflection need not be mainstream or constrained and would indeed benefit from a removal of the mainstream structure imposed on many such endeavours. Opening up creative thought processes through alternative mediums such as expressive art therapy, role play, mask-making and other unique forms of expression will facilitate a new level of communication and expression.

The contradiction here is the inability to resolve conflict internally when we are mandated to support women to resolve conflict. The board needs a clear conflict resolution process that encourages lively, open and honest debate and maintains respect for individuals and differences. Within women's organizations, this conflict resolution process needs to be on paper, everyone needs a copy, and it needs to be reviewed and practised. We are not good at this. Conflict is the one common denominator in all organizations that everyone interviewed agreed is done poorly, destructively or maliciously.

For many women, the initial hurdle is realizing that constructive expressions of anger and other similar emotions are not abusive. Many women find that challenging another woman creates incredible anxiety and is too often confused with being attacked or unsafe. This subtle problem in interpretation leads directly to the core reason why agencies disintegrate. There needs to be an acknowledgement that we must deal with our own oppressive behaviours and attitudes and our emotional history when we are faced with challenges. We need to balance these two concepts at all times when engaging in any conflictual situation.

It is difficult for so many women within this field, regardless of length of their "professional" career, to give and receive feedback in a non-defensive manner. There is not an acknowledgment within the workplace that this is an integral part of anti-violence work. Nor is there an acknowledgement that behaviours that support oppression *must* be challenged — that this is not an option, and is, again, integral to the work itself. There must be created a conflict resolution process that is feminist and anti-racist and that is clear, spelled out and committed to as a condition of employment. *It must be practiced.* Time and funds must be invested in ensuring such a process is applied and understood.

The Role of Political Action
Board members are in the unique and fortunate position that by the nature of their role they are free to engage in political action, to spearhead social change actions and to lobby their heads off. Few board members are even aware of this role, of the necessity of the role or of the politics of why they would be bothered in the first place. They often do not understand this responsibility or desire to engage in such actions.

Without the requisite training and an understanding of the issues of violence against women, boards have no tools or base with which to create a lobby structure or to engage in dialogue concerning political lobby priorities. Lobby committees are imperative to anti-violence work.

Structural power aside, the board does have the ability to hold power in its purest sense. As Jean Baker Miller, in her essay "Women's Growth in Connection," eloquently puts it:

> My own working definition of power is the capacity to produce a change — that is, to move anything from point A or state A to point B or state B. This can even include moving one's own thoughts or emotions, sometimes a very powerful act. It can also include acting to create movement in an interpersonal field, as well as acting in larger realms such as economic, social, or political arenas. (1991: 198)

What About Men?

Okay, to me, it has always been a "no brainer" that there should be no men on the board, but many "feminist" anti-violence agencies have men on their board and actively recruit male board members. At one agency I worked for, the board was women only in practice. A motion went to the membership to include within the by-laws that the board be women only, and the motion was defeated. Men must be involved in our struggle; it is imperative that they are. However, men need to be in supportive roles, and there are plenty of crucial supporting roles. Since we are always struggling for adequate funding, why not fundraise? Donate thousands of dollars? Endorse and espouse our cause at your workplace and campaign for anti-violence agencies to be the recipient of corporate charity money? Speak out publicly on men's violence and its impact? Work at a men's program? There are countless ways to help that would make an enormous impact. But allow women to spearhead our own feminist organizations. We must. To even assume as a man that you should be in any governance role, whether on the board or within a paid position, in my opinion demonstrates that you really do not get the issue anyway!

This is it in a nutshell: women's organizations need to be accountable to the community they serve, and the community is women. Why is the burden of responsibility again on women to abate men's violence while ensuring we involve them? This is such a wolf in sheep's clothing issue, but to react to it in an openly negative way causes a stir even from other women, many of whom are in the anti-violence community. This is a ground for great division; it is fodder for drawing a line in the sand within the feminist community.

There are inherent complications that have the potential to arise when men are included among the female decision-makers. Judith Jordan and her fellow authors do not mince words in describing these issues:

> Although women are not given permission to compete [among each other] the way men are, women are allowed — and even encouraged and groomed — to compete with other women for men. When they compete with men, several problems arise immediately. First is the danger of being considered "'unfeminine," aggressive and destructive — and potentially being called "castrating." Second... some women need to idealize men and see them as stronger and more powerful for the sake of the "rescue fantasy." (Jordan et al. 1991: 231)

> They [women] usually overvalue men, undervalue women, and feel they are lacking something. (Jordan et al. 1991: 225)

MEMBERSHIP

Do you have a membership? Most of the women employed in anti-violence organizations whom I interviewed had no idea whether or not they were indeed legal voting members of their corporation. They also did not know where to look for this information. In fact, the entire non-profit agency structure was a mystery to many.

It is the ethical responsibility of management of anti-violence organizations to educate and inform staff on how the non-profit agency is structured. Keeping staff ill-informed serves no one and is fundamentally contrary to a belief in empowerment of women. Conveying this information is easily done; at a staff meeting, an hour devoted to explaining the ins and outs of non-profit agency governance and management will give all staff a good enough overview to understand the function of personnel and documentation at all levels of the organization. Taking the time to walk women through the structures demonstrates a respect for the staff and provides a common framework on which to build better dialogues internally with regard to policy, accountability and other issues.

It is crucial to understanding what membership means within the organization to convey the importance of having a membership (when possible) to the staff. Is membership promoted internally or is it openly or covertly discouraged? Management needs to promote membership within the organization should that option be available and to advertise when and how memberships can be obtained and renewed.

> *Our agency was being run into the ground. We encouraged women to become members, friends, clients, anyone who had an interest in the direction the agency was going. The administration tried to use various tactics to attempt to deny membership, but we educated women as to their rights according to our by-laws. They expected us to be naïve and complacent. What they got was a coup.* — R

I heard Naomi Wolf speak at Convocation Hall in Toronto with my best friend, who bought me the tickets for my birthday. She was promoting her latest book, *Fire With Fire*. What I most remember her speaking about, with enormous conviction and passion, was women getting off their butts and using their electoral vote. Ensuring that women were campaigned for and elected into office; ensuring their agendas were put forward; using the gender majority. I was not ready to hear this at the time. I was still fairly wet behind the ears in regard to the feminist movement. I still exalted in my oppression and victimization. I could not hear the truth in what she was saying and found myself spouting off reasons why this was a nice theory but not realistic... blah blah blah. Now I hear the same words coming from my own lips.

We continue to underestimate our ability to make change. We are too often apathetic rather than ensuring we are doing all we can to change things. Women are the voting majority: in an article in the *Toronto Star,* the Liberal government tossed out a "warning" to the current Tory government that they'd better start kissing up to women. Voting strategically is a prime example of taking this form of power into our hands. Amazingly again, so many women I spoke to told me that their agencies forbade them to speak of strategic voting even to their clients. Non-partisan politics aside, call a goat a goat. Fighting for our welfare and political voice should not be silenced by the very organizations that stand to lose and be obliterated.

Start now with the women and girls who use your services. Talk about power and politics. Distribute information about systems and how to work them. Develop programs that focus on these types of assertiveness and self improvement. Learn to write a motion. Remember, your clients can lobby, protest and picket. Give them the skills and confidence to do so.

You need to k now the organization. Learn and teach other women how to read and understand financial statements. Spread the power of financial savvy. Finance committees of the board tend also to be renegade committees because they have the tendency to direct. Combine this with a man in the role of treasurer, and thus chair of this committee, and you have established a very unhealthy power dynamic.

Annual general meetings are public forums. Do you go? The premise of non-profits is that they are a response to community need. They receive community money via taxes morphed into transfer payments through a branch of the government, generally provincial. Because non-profits operate with community funds, they require the presence of a community board of directors — a group of volunteers who are ideally representative of the community to oversee the agency and represent the community within the agency. Anyone can go to an annual general meeting of a not-for-profit agency. We need advocates on the boards, and we need allies for those advocates. Annual general meetings provide a forum to permit healthy stacking of board members, the opportunity to challenge the direction of the agency. Gender aside, what are your organization's requirements for membership? What do they need to be?

THE EXECUTIVE DIRECTOR

> With the establishment of a relationship of oppression, violence has already begun. — Paulo Freire

With no tools of our own, we are using old patriarchal frameworks for human resources and management. They are not appropriate for a feminist agency. The executive directors become the patriarchs, and we all enter into the psychodrama role play with one another.

> The feminist or woman focused philosophy rooted in an aware-
> ness of oppression is not something that is easily taught yet it is
> at the fulcrum for the work done and decisions made in a woman
> focused environment. This suggests that ideology and philosophy
> can never be compromised.... The executive director is expected
> to act as the leader of the organization and cannot be seen to be
> struggling with this fundamental value. Anti-violence agencies are
> unique organizations and require unique leadership approaches.
> (Richardson 2001: 72)

Some executive directors pretend to be feminists. Generally, staff see through such pretence but these administrators are not necessarily dismissed from their position. Some are openly unapologetic about not coming from a feminist position.

> *When I wasn't hired for a position as an executive director, I requested*
> *a meeting to ask why. During this discussion, I was told by three board*
> *members that the board didn't feel it necessary to hire managers with*
> *a feminist analysis. They felt this "skill" was only required by front line*
> *staff. Managers were there to be bureaucrats. — R*

It is a contradiction in terms for a feminist agency to have no feminist direction or analysis from its leadership. If anything, it is the managers who should not only lead internally and externally, but who should provide training and direction for new and junior staff. This is before pointing out the obvious: how does a manager without a feminist analysis effectively develop policy, strategic planning, team development and leadership, and a reflective external voice for anti-violence work?

With the demise of the collective, which women within the anti-violence movement saw as the natural and ideal structure to complement our work, many woman have resigned themselves to some form of hierarchy (pending, of course, the development of new models!). The buzz words I heard in my research were "participatory hierarchy." Many agencies professed to have this, but none seemed to actually use it. Most women on the front lines I spoke to, and many middle management and supervisors as well, felt that if they had an executive director they could respect, who could bring strong feminist leadership internally and externally, who was open to new ideas, creative and allowed for a great deal of staff input, they would gladly trust such a person to administer the agency properly. Most front-line workers despised administrative tasks and had no interest in doing them, but did however possess a clear vision of what the executive director should be doing and within what framework.

Why not allow for this to occur? If staff helped in creating a job description, all would feel that they were appropriately represented by their executive director. The board would hold her accountable; no one's thunder would be stolen and everyone would be clear on their roles.

We have not worked long enough at developing the model of what a feminist executive director should be — her boundaries, values, personal experience and education. Boards of directors inevitably fall prey to the familiarity of bureaucracy and patriarchal administration when hiring for this position. The result is the creation of a glaringly patriarchal and often abusive working environment, in which the executive director governs without new inspiration and follows the corporate path. She pays for good legal advice and utilizes it. She governs without participation and clutches her policies and procedures. She is devoid of creativity.

One agency whose executive director was afraid to come out as a lesbian had dynamics of fear and secrecy. She was aware of trying to fit into an old girls' club that had existed within the community for years and that was rather mainstream. Staff were reluctant to be honest and open regarding many issues. Communication tended to be vague and indirect. You get caught up into the role you're playing, caught into the male context of "professionalism."

There are those who escape to management as a distraction from their own problems. Many agencies have leaders who are in states of personal crisis that rival their clients'. This is not to say that women cannot live lives within this work — quite the opposite — but it does appear that some choose management within these agencies to escape and deny personal dysfunction. Similarly, some choose management when client work becomes too painful, forgetting that their staff will need them in a parallel relationship. There are those who seek power, finding a niche in a vulnerable world. They can portray a polished external face, and tend to abuse their agency staff. Some staff described blatant homophobia, abuse of power over staff and elitism over clients.

There exists also the executive director who has herself not come to terms with or defined what feminism is within the workplace. There are no opportunities to discuss the concept. Too often the expectation of demonstrating this understanding is that one will bare one's soul, one's own trauma and history of abuse. Having been abused is made a prerequisite of feminist understanding or the vehicle inductees utilize to find common ground with existing staff members who challenge their feminist comprehension. We are all divorced from seeing feminism as a conceptual and lived understanding. This is a set-up. Should you disclose your own victimization — as soon as you offer up that humanity — you are more than the job, and then you are up for grabs. You are up for scrutiny. The debate of feminism becomes personalized. Should you bare your soul too much, over that un-named line, you may be asked to seek help at an external service. We are not willing to help our own. You are either the "giver" or the "needer."

CHAPTER 2

ORGANIZATIONAL OPERATION

INTRODUCTION

> *The practice of hiring management from outside has created a situation in which those in a position of leadership are neither knowledgeable nor willing to learn about a feminist orientation; they have not had front line clinical experience of the issues of violence against women and children and are making decisions that come from a base that is not disclosed to the staff. Front line program staff on the other hand are steeped in feminist understanding and have tremendous expertise. They have consistently continued their program work through various management crises over the years. Frequently they are ignored when it comes to hiring into management positions, their input in what they need in a manager is not sought out and these positions are filled by managers from non-feminist agencies. — B*

The outside hiring of executive directors creates a crisis every couple years as they inevitably move onto easier jobs because they have faced a tremendous and unfair learning curve as well as burnout and vicarious trauma. Furthermore, this practice of outside hiring has created a glass ceiling for staff who want to further their careers; valuable resources are wasted in training paid for by the agency and then not utilized. The message staff receive is "you are not good enough to be a leader in this organization." The effect of continually juxtaposing experienced stable front line staff with inexperienced short-term management staff who are reluctant to draw on staff experience creates a widening credibility gap mixed with anger and frustration, which makes it harder for management to manage because good faith and trust are disappearing (personal interview with B).

A true leader is not one with the most followers but one
who creates the most leaders. — Neale Donald Walsh

Succession Planning

At a conference on creating a healthy workplace, the keynote speaker focused her attention on the ill treatment of middle management: she felt they had by far the worst jobs within any human service organization (Duxbury 2004).

She stated they were treated badly and were the most overworked, in effect making succession planning impossible.

She went on to make an interesting argument. First, she pointed out that of all of those in attendance, in fact all managers, there were no executive directors. This conference was on creating a healthy work environment and the decision-makers were noticeably absent. She also said that unions needed to push for better treatment of managers. It did seem like a strange idea until she pointed out that how managers are treated within the organization is a predictor of how employees are treated.

Succession planning allows for the development of the entire agency. It encourages the nearly extinct notion of working at one place until you retire or die. Succession planning addresses the failure of managers to pay attention to the important rather than the urgent. Time must be put aside to mentor.

Symptoms of Dysfunction

When the administration of an agency begins a pattern of confronting staff and staff engage in a pattern of resistance, the inevitable quiet war begins. The undertones and the malignant themes behind the confrontation will highlight what that agency and therefore its administration most fear.

At one agency, unionized staff decided to have an "action alert," which highlighted homophobia as an issue within the workplace. Obviously this was done to point out what was believed to be specific homophobic practices, but was framed as a general action alert on the general issue. Information was distributed, pins were handed out and a lesbian-positive poster put up. As staff showed up for a staff meeting later that day, they were informed they were facing disciplinary action, sent home without pay, forced to remove the poster and further disciplined. The incident was not open for discussion at the staff meeting, nor was there any investigation into current practices nor changes made or considered to ensure a more inclusive workplace. The administration squashed the staff's efforts. Its members were afraid of confronting their own homophobia.

The obvious question is why, when issues are brought forth, does management not simply listen and mull it over, maybe reflect, ask for more information and seek to change. We expect that of clients, of abusers, of society. We must encourage discussion at staff meetings, invite feedback, ask questions.

When agencies lack superior, respected leaders, there is splitting within the management groupings. The following are some themes that arose in discussions:

- Executive directors and boards override decisions made by middle managers, discrediting them to their staff by pulling the rug out from under their feet.

- Another level of management is created when there is polarity between the executive director and business manager.
- Managers are not informed of board functions.
- Only some managers are given access to board meetings and personnel files.

Often within agencies with a history of management turnover and internal strife, we see managers and staff alike putting each other in the same roles or boxes that reflect past history. This does not allow for any growth at all but feeds into the theme of recreating dysfunctional family dynamics. These dynamics have contributed to the destruction of many anti-violence agencies, collective and hierarchy alike.

> We hated the business manager before we'd even met her. Our own manager allowed us the space to talk about our issues with money and power, personal and at work. It freed us up a bit to at least start a dialogue. — K

Building Organizational Health

In order to manage a feminist anti-violence organization, anyone having structural power must examine power as a concept and grow a deep understanding of use and abuse of power. Anne Bishop notes in *Becoming an Ally* that in an organization "even one person who wants control and uses the methods of 'power-over' can destroy an experiment in consensus methods." In her experience,

> the other members of the group have to chose among three options. The first is to band together in complete unity to resist the person's attempt to take over. In the second case, one or more members lead the resistance, entering into a power struggle, which in turn demands the use of "power over" tactics and ends the cooperative nature of the group. The third is to break up for the time being. (2002: 43)

The third option is where we see anti-violence organizations fall apart.

> The last two women's shelters I've worked with have been very rigid regarding debate/inclusion of alternative ideas. It's been my impression that the hierarchical power structure permits one woman (and her allies) to impose her belief systems on the organization, and debate is not generally permissible. I've noticed that fear seems to play a large role in keeping alternative voices quiet. The power to hire and fire is a powerful tool. Sometimes it makes me sad to see the waste of potential for positive growth that is stifled by fear. — S

Management needs to be the change agent within the organizational culture; it needs to display the behaviour, the direction and the ethics that guide the work environment. Too often, the managers themselves are far too damaged as people to fulfil that role. They lack the fundamentals of feminist theory, the historical framework of violence against women work, the skills to build a team. They were hired or promoted within a patriarchal business framework by boards of directors who also lacked the same core understanding. The hiring is based on skill sets that may be of value to the organization but when divorced from the fundamentals and basic tenants of feminism are quite useless.

Managers need to ensure they get direction from what Linda Druxbury (2004) refers to as the "soul centres" of the organization — those respected individuals within the organization who carry and embody the heart and soul of the place, those who carry the culture. Administration too often gets "everything," meaning newly acquired resources. When things are new and when gains are obtained, they should be given to the "masses" — the front-line workers.

Sometimes there needs to be a healthy mutiny. This is a dangerous tactic but often a necessary one. What we do not need is to be active in dynamics of scapegoating, which in our haste to solve a problem can lead the most well-intentioned group to engage in a witch hunt. It is imperative that specific behaviours and actions be addressed, not the personality of the executive director or manager.

> The only management style that works within a feminist anti-oppression agency is a participatory hierarchy where the executive director and managers and board of directors seek systematic input from staff in all matters of strategic, program, policy and procedure planning and where input is not only sought, but implemented. — K

I would also state that clients must be an instrumental component of any participatory hierarchy. We are not a factory.

To effectively orchestrate a healthy mutiny, ensure that the core group is impenetrable; do not saturate the media; and follow appropriate channels and chains of command.

One of the most eerie similarities between anti-violence workers within their workplace and violence survivors is the degree to which they are hypervigilant of their colleagues and their environment. Front-line staff are generally the most attuned to internal tensions, of which managers often seem oddly unaware. Should management be more attuned to such tensions, they could be instrumental in avoiding much of the meltdown that occurs within organizations. Management could make a plan to address the tension, and do so with creativity and safety. This in fact needs to be its role, although most managers do not acknowledge this as such.

So many of the women I spoke with articulated a degree of fear and of feeling "on edge" when going to work. This sense of peril, this fear of "who's next" came and went in cycles, periods of crisis and periods of relative peace. Sound familiar? The experience of the cycle of violence by abused women and kids is being mirrored with grotesque frequency within anti-violence organizations. Women differ in how they respond to this need to be vigilant of the cycle of scapegoating, of cutbacks, of abuse by management, of racism and homophobia, of the sense of collapse and re-building that is occurring. This may depend on previous victimization or abuse, and in this automatic recreation of previous trauma workers have often found themselves in the roles of counsellor and victim within the same workplace, within the same circle of individuals. Women, who are often so much more attuned with spiritual and emotional changes within a relationship, any relationship, have found themselves exhausted, sick, using substances, acting out, withdrawing, quitting and burning out in countless other ways.

Do not ask for permission: just act. See what can happen if we are operating from good intentions.

It is a short step from accepting hierarchy as natural
to assuming that exploitation is just. — Anne Bishop

For many it seems so simple: if the hierarchal structure were gone, the power would be equally shared. Those women have never worked within a collective structure and witnessed its actual dreadful imbalance of power, which is co-opted in various forms as the structure operates free from any traditional hierarchical model. But the problem with the hierarchical model is that there are very few people who are able to bring feeling into positions imbedded within a power framework; the very structure invites people who are power hungry.

Is it possible that those who hold positions at the "top" of a traditional hierarchical model, those who theoretically hold the power, can espouse a non-hierarchical model that encourages connection, recognizes the importance of a felt sense of safety within the agency and within interpersonal peer relationships, recognizes the power and primacy of relationships for healing and growth, and encourages members to challenge not just one another, but authority — the director herself. This would minimize the power differential between the staff and the director, empowering the staff to grasp opportunities for change and growth as they arise.

The hierarchical structure implemented in women's organizations mirrors the same patriarchal, oppressive model that has created the landscape in which the female staff have been born and socialized. If the model is therefore the re-creation of all the nuances of abusive power, then the relationship established goes beyond one of structural or co-opted power and is transformed into one of abuser and victim.

Generally the relationship between management and staff is not one of intentional abuse and misuse of power. Yet all the elements of the abusive relationship remain, the dynamic that unfolds is much the same as that between abusive partner and his spouse: the abusive partner swears never to use force again and professes willingness to change, and the spouse is eager to believe those promises and minimizes both the truth and inherent pitfalls. Even if both partners desire reconciliation, as Herman puts it:

> their unspoken goals are often sharply in conflict. The abuser usually wishes to re-establish his pattern of coercive control, while the victim wishes to resist it. Though the abuser is often sincere in his promise to give up the use of force, his promise is hedged with implicit conditions; in return for his pledge of non-violence, he expects his victim to give up her autonomy. As long as the abuser has not relinquished his wish for dominance, the threat of violence is still present. The victim cannot speak freely in couple sessions, and the conflictual issues in the relationship cannot possibly be discussed. (1992: 168)

Abusive silencing behaviour exists in women's organizations when staff are not able to challenge, confront and discuss. Although there is no threat of violence upon any individual, there are implicit conditions related to the surrender of autonomy.

> Another way to make man fight and kill is to establish an absolute hierarchy of leadership and to reward only obedience. This will also give the mobility and speed of response required by war. Hierarchical leadership connects back to a number of other circles. The process of teaching people to value obedience must apply to all oppressed people — women, children, slaves. Also, hierarchy and obedience among individuals reinforces the notion of a hierarchy among peoples inherent in racism. (Bishop 2002: 28)

All agencies appear to have policies that address insubordination, a concept floating adrift within feminist anti-violence organizations without context or direct purpose (an example of copying male models without rethinking old constructs). The policies are never or rarely used for any disciplinary purpose; their sole purpose is to be inserted into collective agreements and policy binders. The notion of insubordination itself implies a failure to adhere to rigid hierarchy, and its existence is in total contrast to the fight against power and control.

Just as there exist (or should exist) counselling models within agencies that espouse a feminist counselling framework, there also needs to be a documented administrative model that follows a feminist framework. This model needs to be developed and embraced by the entire agency and adopted into board level and operating polices. All administrative decision-making and day-to-day operating must fall from this framework, to which management is accountable.

Feminist Structures and Feminist Models

Adopting mainstream management models limits how we work; it's constraining and archaic. We are scared of giving way; we have a fear of collaboration. It might mean losing ourselves somehow, our jobs, our identity. We have acted this out by not playing nicely with other shelters. We will not give our place up to a woman of colour, not in reality, and we only tout this as rhetoric when appropriately pressed.

> Powerlessness is a common theme for workers and clients alike. The literature contrasts the worker's desire for a sense of power and control with systemic unpredictability. This approach perpetuates the assumption that one holds power over another: the management over the workers and the workers over the clients. It promotes "we-they" thinking and fails to explore avenues for individual and collective empowerment. (Finn 1990: 62)

The world we live in does not value consensus decision-making, and it is difficult therefore to implement into the workplace. When I first began the work of violence against women as paid work, I was indoctrinated into the world of collectives. The first three agencies I worked in all operated this way, and I was thrilled to witness the operationalizing of this strand of feminist ideology. Of course, I was only a relief worker, so I did not have to go to staff or board meetings, and I was blissfully unaware of the underlying dynamics and politics that lay beneath the surface. Of course I felt them on occasion, but chose to remain happily oblivious. Then I was hired along with five other women to establish a new centre, one with a collective structure, and got my first and most powerful lesson in the dynamics of "horizontal aggression." We were fighting to have power and failed to notice that we already had it. Perhaps the most heinous misuse of power is to pretend you do not have any.

The collective structure and the related dysfunction that plays itself out within a supposed framework of social equality is a result of engaging in a hierarchical structure without naming it. We take roles on and then are forced into denial because we need confirm to the world that we are indeed powerless. If we acknowledge the power imbalance within the collective, we negate our own structure, which we see as visionary. If we acknowledge the power imbalance within the collective structure, we are forced to examine the dysfunctional manner in which women handle conflict and the link with our imbedded societal "roles."

Having no structure of our own, no feminist models for running agencies, we adapt poorly to the same structures that have oppressed us.

> A time honoured feminist ideal of group organization, which came out of the early feminist criticism of men's meetings as domineering, ego-driven, and rigidly hierarchical events.... Since consensus involved hearing from everyone, our level of irritation with one another rose exponentially as we all inflicted increasingly acute boredom on one another. (Wolf 1994: 154)

It is a daunting task to find mechanisms to accommodate others' ideas, when our structure, our larger societal structure, does not value consensus and requires enforcement of timelines and deadlines.

> *We were all expected to have input, and this would ensure we all had a voice. Yet so many of us apologised or made some sad disclaimer prior to everything we said, that it seemed like a mockery. — G*

> *Then someone started using the "most oppressed" card to garner power. Obviously it worked, we were all too scared, too white, too straight, too privileged, to naïve, too chicken, too blind to call her on it. Looking back, we should have acknowledged her feelings and as a group deconstructed it. But we acquiesced and got on with the business at hand. — D*

Surely to god, if we get enough women in one room and give us some wine, we could develop something at least a little better than what we've got. Women's organizations parallel religious intention versus religious structure. We have accepted the religious (as it finds merit in structure), but have rejected the spiritual, the very core of what should be religious.

We must tap into the "soul centres" of the organization — those individuals who are the heart and soul of the organization and who have their finger on the pulse of all that is going on. We need to build trust with these women and use them for climate checks and as advisors.

> The majority felt tyrannized by the minority, the minority felt overruled by the majority, and the happy face of complete agreement in public was betrayed by a frenzy of back stabbing in tiny Machiavellian groups as soon as we were out of the room. These "alliances," of course, were unreliable, as you always knew you could be vivisected in turn. (Wolf 1994: 155)

Naomi Wolf (1994) posits an interesting idea that women should create a new form of social organization, complementing the grassroots activist group and the "power group." The power group, as she frames it, would be akin to affiliation groups, similar to the ones white women belonged to that fostered the actions for winning women the vote. Wolf suggests that the creation of a power group fosters a comfortable community while developing "a new psychology of power and consolidated female clout."

Wolf is also clear that women are nervous about the idea of consolidating power in affiliation groups because such groups suggest elitism or exclusiveness. "But the fact is that women do have different agendas, backgrounds, and interests" (Wolf 1994: 296). Such is the paradox at the centre of much of the strife within the culture of women's organizations: an acknowledgement of our differences as women, along race, class and ethnicity lines, and the resultant variety of agendas and philosophies, while simultaneously we've been beating our heads against the wall trying to create one service, one type of organization that will encompass all these differences and also deliver service that is reflective of all these differences. At the same time we juggle consensus decision-making, struggle away from old models and search for a common voice with which to present *women* to the world as a unified group — the impossible task of creating sameness within difference.

Wolf highlights the benefits of her proposed structure in creating a feminism that is fun and lucrative, creates community, eases women's anxieties around power and changes women's views of other women (as resources and repositories of power, not competitors). In her words, "We must replace the sentimentalized model of sisterhood with a pragmatic model" (301).

RECRUITING AND KEEPING THE RIGHT STAFF

As the workforce decreases, it is becoming increasingly difficult to attract and retain the right staff. It is a seller's market for those who are job hunting; highly skilled women are harder to attract especially when your organization is not located in an urban centre, and when nearly every other non-profit organization can offer better compensation. The focus of hiring must be recruitment *and* retention.

Clear job descriptions must capture the nuances of what we do and include the feminist framework we are supposed to espouse. In advertising externally for job vacancies the wording of the ad must be proud of and open about a feminist framework.

Interviews need to move away from consisting of pat, tight questions, which always require the obligatory "define feminism," which prompts the "textbook" right answer. Interviews need to focus on eliciting responses that will help you to know the woman you are interviewing. Begin to make the links at the outset that this work is a very internal process; the functions may appear external, but the process is internal, and seek an inventory of the interviewee's emotional well-being linked to a feminist understanding of where they are at.

We need to train staff. We need to look at such training in a creative light; we are not imposing rules and practices upon staff but integrating them into our joint core values. We are not tossing the policy manual at them. A consultant said to me, "I am so surprised; given your role as a manager, why you aren't upset when staff are late?" I said, "I know they are going to be late. I schedule things to begin a half an hour after I tell them they are starting." "And that doesn't bother you? No attendance management policies?" As always I shudder at the thought. I explained that these women will put in countless hours of unpaid overtime, they will do research at home, they will support one another in countless ways after normal work hours. It has become apparent to me that women in this field are always late, so why fight it? Why set up a pugilistic relationship? We can work around it and everyone retains their dignity; we are all aware of what the problem is and have found creative ways to deal with it respectfully. Focus on the strengths of what that employee does well.

Rigid policy sets up a dynamic of fear and control, rather than accountability. Setting up this dynamic causes resentment of the distrust demonstrated by the bureaucracy and will backfire with an unhealthy shift in attitude. We need to be cognizant of our use of language in all aspects of our work, even with what might seem a benign form, because of the nature of the agency and overarching belief systems that guide us. A form may not be just a form, it may have implications and may be internalized in many ways by a group of women, marginalized by gender, who hail from the many backgrounds that afford us a greater sensitivity in doing this work. In a profession where there is such a high degree of vicarious trauma and burnout, our energies need to be focused on keeping staff together, not tearing them apart. Allow employees to explore what they are good at. If they develop an interest, such as political action, find ways to channel this. Allow for freedom within the job to try new things.

We also need to be cognizant of these issues when we attempt to build agency esteem and community "image" by moving away from staff diversity to standardization and accreditation. Let's think through this push toward the bachelor of social work.

The anti-violence movement has fought against this pressure for years, for many reasons I will delve into, and they are as relevant today (perhaps even more so) since the move toward "accreditation" is found within the same organizations that once rallied against it. The trend among executive directors is to post jobs listing a BSW as a preferred qualification, to encourage staff to seek registration within associations and to "professionalize" their staff.

Perhaps they feel the state-sponsored influence of the child welfare folks, who are standardized but who also receive training sponsored by their agency. A contributing factor may be devaluing comments made by misogynists lingering within such systems as the judicial system, who question anti-violence workers' abilities and "credentials."

> There are also signs of a shift away from community-based, independent women's counselling and advocacy. Recently, the Ministry of Health has moved to professionalize emotional counselling under the Regulated Health Professions Act. This measure seriously affects the support and counselling currently offered by Rape Crisis/Sexual Assault Centres. (Khosla 2003: 17)

Really, let us see much of this for what it is — misogyny and classism.

I was at a meeting and listened to a group of front-line children's workers who ran specific group programs speaking about their groups and tossing out words like "therapy" and "assessment." We launched into a discussion about the need to accurately portray what we do: not to minimize our service or abilities, but to ward off the standardization dragon that comes in the form of social work accreditation. Certain terms are linked to the BSW, which we fought in order to embrace diversity and experience. This is the caution in professionalization: we once again remove ourselves another step from the women we serve, create a further "us and them" scenario — us with the degree and them with the problem..

A beautiful book, *Women's Ways of Knowing* (Belenky et al. 1997) seeks an understanding of how women come to know and learn through the social institutions of school and family, both of which strive to instruct growing girls on how they should experience and "be" in the world. Embracing the forms in which a woman learns and experiences the world is essential in appropriately weighing the ability of that woman to perform the role of anti-violence counsellor or advocate. Narrowing perspectives on what are deemed acceptable standards for work in this field is nothing less than establishing a set of final learned outcomes — a virtual impossibility in a human services field. Are we not all learning on a continuum? Standardization of skills, education and ability and accreditation will only serve to further mainstream and white privilege an "inclusive service."

Our interviewing and human resources management rarely reflect learning, true learning, styles of learning, or life experiences. As we as counsellors wade through the lives of others and attend staff meetings and do case management and supervision, there is no reflection of the uniqueness of women's sense of the world and how all the dramas she witnesses unfolding become part of her growth and part of herself. For the most part, managers, hired on the basis of mainstream criteria, or their espousal of mainstream human resource management, fail to look beyond the presentation of those staff that challenge or confuse and combat their own insecurity with constructs and work plans in a desperate attempt to impose a framework. Women of diverse backgrounds, women, for example, whose primary language is not English, may be lost within such tasks and fail to meet the manager's expectations. These same women may possess invaluable skills but are without the safety or support to utilize them.

Belenky et al. argue that true multicultural, gendered discourse could be built on "pedagogies of positionality," using constructed knowing as a "jumping off place, not a final destination." The problem with examining truths with only a gender framework, albeit an essential one, is that it does not allow for distinctions within that gender — of class, race, ethnicity, sexual orientation and so on. This is one of the reasons why women of colour had to rally against the white feminist movement. It did not represent them. The constructs of gender, though valid for the most part, were devoid of the experience of colour and race. What was constructed was hollow, substanceless and just not accurate.

Well, this destroyed the white folk. Struggling against patriarchy and securing some small successes and then realizing that *all* women were not unified to their cause. What manifests are stronger ideologies from those women who have been left out of the framework and who have experienced oppression differently.

> The proliferation of such standpoint feminisms represented a new set of problems, namely, those generated by the implications of a series of parallel "knowledges" that existed alongside each other without intersecting, or being able to claim knowledge of each other except as regards those experiences held in common. The results have been the stalemates of "identity politics," where members of different dominated and exploited groups, in trying to understand who they are, struggle against the barriers between them and other groups that these same identities create. (Goldberg at al. 1998: 156)

The sensitivity to differences in gender, a lens through which to examine power, authority, voice, victimization and dominance, must be applied within women's organizations. We would love to expect this in the outside world, so why have we failed to change how we facilitate staff meetings, engage in performance appraisals, "discipline'" and structure our physical and emotional working environments? The answer lies very much entrenched in white feminism and the stagnation of the norms created internally in white women's agencies.

Changing the "identity politics" that arise from the struggle with binary oppositions (men/women, black/white) has been achieved only through the relaxation of white women in their vigilance to not hear the truths in the experiences of women of colour. Acceptance of these truths can allow for integration of multiple identities and an "emphasis on the constructedness, through shifting language, discourse, and histories of all 'identities'" (Goldberg et al. 1998: 156). Viewing identities as multiple sparked "post-modern feminists" to "look at these terminologies as markers of false dichotomies, and to uncover the relations of power and domination they mask" (Goldberg et al. 1998: 156). Taking this more global approach permits the expression of the stories and experiences of all women in an unfragmented, holistic manner, with less emphasis on positioning and without further creating an "us and them" environment. This is not to take the focus off of the individual, but rather to enhance the picture of that individual to gain a better understanding and a more respectful relationship.

Within the shelter or sexual assault centre workplace environment, this approach encompasses the uniqueness of all staff, not only in who they are (viewed by themselves and by others), but in terms of how they see their work and the purpose in what they do — how they see their clients, how they see the systems their clients struggle within, how they learn, how they respond to "supervision," how they behave in a group. It is crucial that each woman within the workplace is truly "seen" and known. Only if there exists a security in the existence of self within the whole can there be a functional team.

Mainstreaming and benchmarking narrow specific criteria for "belonging" and employability not only grossly narrows the window through which to view the individual, but creates a false microcosm of women who can and should be doing this work. It becomes a trout farm, instead of a living lake. Taking into account the differences in the way women think:

> I have learned that like many women, I speak and think in a multi modal, spiral way using both hemispheres of my brain and the intelligence of my body all at the same time.... In most women, the corpus callosum, the part of the brain that connects the right and left hemispheres, is thicker than it is in most men. That is, male and female brains are "wired" differently. Men characteristically use mostly their left hemispheres to think and to communicate their thoughts; their reasoning is usually linear and solution-oriented. It gets to "the point." Women in contrast, recruit more areas of the brain when they communicate than do men. They use the right and left sides of their brain. Because the right hemisphere has richer connections with the body than the left hemisphere, women have more access to their body wisdom when speaking and thinking than do most men. (Northrup 1994: 32–33)

One of the most profoundly disturbing things is the deeply ingrained myth of "professionalism" regarding survivor work. The founding "mothers" of one sexual assault centre had instilled a very elitist and psychiatrized view of counselling sexual assault survivors. This tight core group of women had deemed that only a master of social work (MSW) with a specific formal training (apprenticeship) with the founding matrons would be an adequate and responsible basis upon which to even apply for the counsellor position. What resulted, naturally, and I assume with some premeditation, is that only this core group of women were deemed "qualified" to work with survivors of sexual assault and abuse. This created a manufactured hierarchy of qualification and status within the anti-violence community. These women blocked staff who wished to apply, who would have been more than suitable, under the guise of their lack of "qualifications." This perpetuated the stigma appointed to survivors in so many other arenas: that they were sick and required specialized care — expert care — MSW care. Worse, one of the "requirements" was that the woman as counsellor could not have been a survivor herself, that somehow this background made her inept and unable to counsel a women with the same experience.

The recruitment ad must be clear. It must reflect the norms of the agency and spell out the expectation of feminist analysis. For the entire agency there must be a constant pursuit of increased learning, but those in the position of hiring must ensure that a base from which to build is present. Otherwise, mainstream will breed mainstream. Those without the analysis will enter into positions in which they can influence hiring and will hire other mainstream employees. This point is absolutely crucial in hiring into management positions, which by their nature exert greater power. Soft peddling of the ad in order to attract more résumés will only serve to create a more time-consuming process of short-listing applicants and this will waste resources. Do not unconsciously feed into self-doubt and public shame by putting your logo and agency in the paper with a job description that does not demand a feminist analysis. The following phrase illustrates what is needed: "Possess a thorough understanding and support of a feminist analysis of the issue of violence against women and the ability to integrate feminist theory into management administration." A disturbing trend uncovered when speaking to agency staff is the alteration of job descriptions after the initial posting in order to justify the hiring of unqualified staff or to cover up or justify an agenda in hiring a specific candidate. The job description must also be strong and clear about the expectation that the candidate will *maintain and enhance* a feminist analysis.

During interviews, we all ask the same stupid old question: "What is your definition of feminism?" without knowing what it is we want to hear. Everyone in the room probably has their own interpretation of it anyway, so how can there be a standard by which to "grade" a response? Interviews are too structured. There is no room for a woman to simply talk about herself and why she wants to work at a given agency. A looser approach allows for different styles of responses, helps those who have trouble with interviews and those who may rebel against the structure of them, and also assists women who do not have English as their first language.

Given the right compensation, women will work in this field as a career. And it should be the case that it is a lifestyle even more than a career. An important strategy for keeping great women in this field and for attracting other women to the anti-violence field and to feminism is demonstrating what they can and will get out of it — making the women's movement fun and exciting to be a part of.

> The staff are more than a cornerstone of the operation, in many ways they are the service.... The agencies and buildings are empty shells without the diversity, compassion and commitment of the staff. Staff often chose to work with assaulted and abused women, children and their abusers because they have a particular expertise and desire to make a difference. (Richardson 1991: 74)

We need to take burnout seriously. When burnout occurs, the problem is the structure, and the organization must change. "Much of the literature suggests that the solution to burnout is self-preservation and adaptation in an unhealthy environment" (Finn 1990: 64). Many strategies and suggestions have been put forward about decreasing burnout. In the anti-violence field, it appears that administration is often reticent to implement even the most obvious and simple cosmetic solutions, they can therefore never begin to address the more substantive and crucial organizational changes. As Finn points out, a feminist approach to burnout requires a holistic view.

> Both workers and clients are part of a larger system that has historically valued power, autonomy, and competition over mutual support, affiliation, and the equitable distribution of resources.... Therefore, cosmetic solutions make the ties of the welfare bind less abrasive without confronting the core dilemma of the bind itself. (Finn 1990: 65)

However, as all workers interviewed agreed, some cosmetic solutions would be nice. This type of change would at least demonstrate an agency's good faith towards staff and a willingness to examine the structural issues. What follows is a list of common stumbling blocks noted by a wide cross-section of individuals working within this sector.

Alternative Work Hours or Flex-Time: Many of the women I spoke with worked for agencies that did not espouse flexible hours or alternative schedules. Ironically, most of these agencies had programs that ran on a twenty-four-hour basis, such as emergency shelters. These agencies were inflexible about creative ways of dividing up those non-standard hours, despite the requirement that staff be available for all shifts within the twenty-four-hour period. Programs that ran on a more standard "nine to five" basis still offered no access to alternative hours or flex-time, again despite the demand on staff to perform functions such as group facilitation outside of the nine to five schedule.

In several cases administration offered the explanation that many staff worked part-time and viewed the employment contract of part-time hours as equivalent to flex-time. These agencies were completely resistant to permitting part-time staff (and for the most part full-time staff) to develop a flexible schedule. Policies disallowed this type of creative movement with hours and promoted a hard-core rigidity within scheduling.

Legislative and workplace recognition that flex-time policies are beneficial and in fact, productivity-promoting seem oddly resisted within feminist organizations, where many women have numerous responsibilities outside the office. Linda Duxbury, a sociologist and work/life conflict expert at Carleton University says "legislation is necessary, but it's not the whole answer. We also need a cultural shift. Employers need to stop evaluating employees in terms of how many hours they work, and start looking at a person's output" (Duxbury 2004).

What I found in my own work experience was an attitude of scepticism and distrust towards the idea of flex-work schedules — a sentiment that employees were "cheating" and not working their compensated hours, and a clear resentment towards those employees who managed to have some degree of control of their own scheduling. This mistrust also extended to these employees' direct supervisors, who were often viewed as "soft" on their staff and not "managing" them. Of course this dynamic then leaked into team division and created dissention within the management structure, creating the good/bad manager scenario.

This same attitude was applied to the notion of working at home — which is an equally progressive and accommodating arrangement that has the potential to create a staff team of healthy, long-term employees — even in the face of relevant technology and the ease of creating "virtual offices."

Subsidized Daycare: How hard is it to pay for some spots for all your staff with children? Or allow childcare on site? Shelters are already equipped with childcare spaces and child witness programs.

Pensions: Women devoted to this field are rewarded by retirement into poverty; this is antithetical to the purpose driving this work.

50

Help Women Build Wealth: Organizations need to devote effort to this end via workshops, training, programs and scholarships.

Employee Assistance Programs: Many women's organizations no longer have employee assistance programs because they are deemed too costly. The reason these programs become overused is often a direct fallout from internal mismanagement.

Proper and Appropriate Clinical Supervision and Debriefing: Two things: understand that the process of staff supervision *is* therapy, and the process of supervision must mirror what is going on and expected at the front line with clients. Not providing such support creates a liability for the agency.

> *If program staff burn out and are not adequately supported, this vicarious trauma spreads to management and support staff and creates an unhealthy environment all over, which leads to a crisis in the entire agency. — H*

Give All Employees the Same Benefits: Do not have some staff working nineteen hours a week, avoiding having to pay them benefits and treating them like second-class citizens. Agencies do this as a cost-saving measure, which leads to the establishment of a classist system within the organization. Our agencies offer little else but poor compensation to poor women. At least allow them the dignity of visiting the dentist.

Use Women/Staff for Their Personal Skills: Do not force staff to conform to what you think they should be doing and the skill base you think they should have. Get to know your staff well enough to creatively place them in roles in which they will flourish. In return for being enthusiastic in their work, they might just stay and reduce the high turnover rate.

Do Not Insult Us: The women I interviewed stated that the organizations for which they worked acted in an administrative fashion that was both silly and deeply insulting. Here are some examples:

> *I have worked in this field for eighteen years. I have been with this agency for eight years. I moved into a new position and my manager who has been in this field for six months put me on probation for six months. — K*

> *I worked as a counsellor here for twelve years. I applied internally for another position, another counselling position in another program. They put me through the interview process as if I were new to the agency. It was humiliating. — BH*

"Congratulations on your new job. You are required to have a physical assessment from your doctor to confirm your capability of performing the job." It was the same job I had been doing for ten years. Management "re-classified" and inserted this requirement to try and fire people. So much for ableism? — BW

Allow for Joy: The feminist workplace needs to be a touchstone for rejuvenation. Many women feel odd, uncomfortable and afraid to laugh at work.

Give Women a Sense of Feeling Valued: People will put up with a lot if they feel valued. This is pertinent both to the individual and to the team. When one individual "isn't good enough," the whole team tends to absorb the sense of not being good enough and members lash out. This is a situation in which all the links in the chain need to support the weakest link.

Days Away/Retreats: This will be discussed in greater detail further on. From what I have ever seen, this is by far the most effective tool for team cohesion, self-care and internal growth for women who experience vicarious trauma.

Distribute Information: Reluctance or laziness in disseminating information results in breakdown of trust and transparency, which is necessary for effective operations. Information is power and it has to be shared.

The grapevine grows most vigorously in organizations where secrecy, poor communication by management and autocratic leadership behaviours are found. — Jan Richardson

---

Don't deny or Withhold Basic Securities: Do not hold back pay; ensure that staff have their paycheque and then figure out mistakes from there. There is all too often a classist notion that employees should somehow manage financially despite interruption in their pay. The reality is that the vast majority of employees in this field are single-income reliant, living paycheque to paycheque and without the luxury of savings. These employees are already wildly underpaid, and most have no financial stability offered to them by their organization.

Celebrations: We need to punctuate when good things happen.

Faith: Work with women's value base and have faith in their abilities.

Discuss Our Own Oppression and Our Role in this Oppression: Without permitting women space to discuss their own experience with oppression, we can never move to honest dialogue about our involvement in oppression, our own roles as oppressors. Anne Bishop outlines the following six steps involved in what she terms "becoming an ally":

1. understanding oppression, how it came about, how it is held in place, and how it stamps its pattern on the individuals and institutions that continually recreate it;
2. understanding different oppressions, how they are similar, how they differ, how they re-enforce one another;
3. consciousness and healing;
4. becoming a worker for your own liberation;
5. becoming an ally; and
6. maintaining hope.

These principles are fundamental in working with marginalized women and maintaining a healthy, non-oppressive work environment.

FINANCIAL MATTERS

We need to explore feminist business theory: Business practices and ethics within a feminist framework. If this is indeed possible, we need to work aggressively to develop such a model and incorporate it into our agencies, just as we would a feminist counselling model and, as I have suggested, a feminist administrative model. This model obviously needs to be predicated upon feminist theory with unique sensitivity to class and race. It must then be put on paper and distributed throughout the agency, all agency employees trained in its application, and the model also made transparent to the community and those in businesses with which the agency deals.

> Accountability all too often is focused on budgets and internal control mechanisms such as policies, rather than on clients. A feminist approach demands that we challenge the acceptance of product over process and re-evaluate the helping relationship accordingly. We need to question the amount of stress that stems not from the nature of the helping process, but from the arbitrary imposition of demands for predictability and control. (Finn 1990: 61)

Those holding leadership positions within the agency must possess the feminist framework first. They can be trained on the financial and business end of things. Board after board falls into this serious error — hiring an executive director for what it believes to be the proper business background and bureaucratic skills only to watch her flounder when she cannot grasp the feminist framework. "It is difficult to have an individual learn an attribute or belief (such as a feminist philosophy) versus a skill (such as conflict resolution or financial management)" (Richardson 1991: 72).

All organizational decisions and policies or procedures must flow from this feminist business theory base. It is apparently not enough to assume that if the agency espouses a feminist mission statement it will actually behave in harmony with those sentiments. Nowhere is this more glaring than when it comes to financial management and business-related matters. I have heard of and seen countless degrading and demeaning practices stringently adhered to on the backs of counsellors, who must then conduct themselves within the guidelines of the feminist framework, wondering why they feel so bloody awful. Women who hold the purse strings of the agency must have the greatest skill and decorum of all; they must be always aware of their power.

> *The agency made a mistake on my pay. They decided to correct that mistake by withholding the overpayment all at once. It was Christmas. I received no money at all. They never even told me. When I confronted her [the business manager] she acted as though she were the victim. She later filed a complaint against me because I was angry when I spoke to her. — L*

All policies and operating practices must originate purely to create the maximum dignity for the women they affect. They must be created and consistently reviewed from a place of constant vigilance and awareness of the power and control issues behind money and wealth.

As an agency, we need to dialogue about how we as women are paid: not merely the compensation itself, but the mechanisms. How do we process mistakes? How do we solicit tenders? How do we screen subcontractors? How do we deal with money-related crises with clients? How do we fundraise and from whom will we solicit and accept money?

Are we clear on whose money we will take and do we have a policy? Fundraising too cannot be divorced from the model to which the agency is accountable. There needs to be agreement across the agency on what are acceptable fundraising initiatives and discussion about what that agency's norms will be, what they can accept in order to sustain themselves while not compromising their mission and mandate. For example, many organizations operate using money donated by casinos or accept proceeds from fashion shows. Without transparent norms, there will be dissent within the staff group when a fundraising initiative is viewed as contravening the agency's philosophy. The fundraiser must be given clear guidelines and must operate within them.

I remember reading an article in *Canadian Geographic* about an initiative designed to protect endangered rams from over-hunting, which opened up a competition where the winners, who paid a large fee, were permitted to hunt these endangered animals within a prescribed quota. The fees were used to assist with protecting the larger herd of rams.

I couldn't help but imagine a fundraiser for women's anti-violence agencies that permitted a violent act within confined parameters in order to obtain the fee paid by the offender which would then provide services to protect victims. On a seemingly more benign scale, this is the difficulty many women have with donations from perpetrators and fashion shows. Without group discussion and a rationale behind the fundraising decision-making, these women are left feeling uneasy, as though there has been a sell-out.

The Funding Dilemma

If we look at the funding structure of Legal Aid Ontario and the community-based legal clinics they fund, we find that Legal Aid Ontario is an independent statutory corporation through which money flows from the Attorney General. This central-funder structure permits these clinics to operate autonomously, since often they are in battle with other extensions of the same government that is funding them. This independence allows the community board to decide the focus of its clinic and gives the community more ownership of that clinic. If provincial ministries of Community and Social Services (MCSS) did the same, local shelter boards could decide to use dollars for outreach, etc. and tailor-make programs for their communities.

The other benefit is that the Ontario Association of Interval and Transition Houses (OAITH), the Ontario Coalition of Rape Crisis Centres and similar bodies in Ontario and other provinces could be funded at arm's length. Realistically, all agencies should earmark fundraising dollars for the specific purpose of sustaining themselves by sustaining their provincial associations.

When the ministry is pushing for a number-crunching approach in its service evaluation, the only antidote is a strong board of directors. To have such strong boards, those women who comprise it must be knowledgeable about the issues, the herstory of the movement and social justice issues. Compliance with governmental regulation and restriction can be approached much more creatively by a committed board representative of its community, supported by networks and coalitions. Now is the time for women with wealth to present themselves as matrons for the future of their daughters' well-being. A group of wealthy supporters would permit a beautiful freedom of service delivery and social justice and political action.

It is also time to step up to the plate as individuals within the work. As employees, we likely do not have cash on hand to support our organizations apart from meagre monetary and labour donations. Believe in the cause enough to will money from your "estate" and to request that money go to your organization in lieu of flowers. This is also an opportunity to designate where these funds would go, specifically to social justice work rather than administrative costs, for example, a freedom not allowed in many agencies where donated dollars go into a general fund to cover operating deficits.

Perhaps the dysfunction within many organizations is manifesting what we already know: that current models and practices may be outdated and ineffective. Perhaps now is the time to return to the days of true grassroots collective action, be beholden to no one and just go about getting the job done. No more nickel-and-dime board-driven fundraising. It is time to get inventive, provocative and creative. Be bold with your fundraising, shameless in your brainstorming. The Vagina Monologues was just the beginning. I saw so many mild mannered "ladies" laughing their asses off. It gave them a chance to be real.

It is time to sell our resources. Many agencies have done this, but tend to market only to other anti-violence agencies, which are financially strapped as well. We offer incredible group curriculum and anti-bullying programs, to name a few. Market these to those with more money, not only to offset costs but to sustain a portion of the fundraising requirement.

Women's organizations have a wealth of information they can pass on. We can sell corporate training packages and create fee for service agreements.

Governments and funders have co-opted the term "victim" in order to make women's services part of the mainstream. We have witnessed this in victim assistance and victim witness programs, which espouse gender neutrality and nullify the reality of femicide, patriarchal oppression and misogyny. This amalgamation makes the definition of victim so benign that there can be no argument made for specialized services.

The pendulum has swung from gales of laughter in the House of Commons when the issue of wife assault was put on the table back in the early 1980s to the dismantling of governmental departments with any degree of influence or power that had women's issues as their primary focus. Wow, it only took a twenty-year cycle to be given blood money and have it taken away. It is shameful and unconscionable that this has occurred after our society had awakened and acknowledged the truths of women abuse.

Canadian provincial governments are systematically wiping out all women's policy units in a disturbing display of bureaucratic misogyny. Women's directorates and secretariats play a vital role in reviewing and developing government legislation. Policy analysis crafts new initiatives and improves existing programs. It is easy to foretell that with such antagonism toward these quality units, women will cease to have a voice and women's progress will deteriorate, beginning at the provincial level and eventually influencing federal thinking.

As the Yukon dismantled its Women's Directorate policy unit on April Fool's Day of 2002, an e-mail sent by the Yukon Status of Women Minister (yes, a woman) was quoted in several newspapers declaring the women's movement dead and referring to women's groups as "feminazis" who had taken over her right to state her opinions. It is easy to see which women are allowed into the political arena and why. It is easy to see what is coming down the pipe.

In 2001 the Liberal government in British Columbia dismantled the Ministry of Women's Equality and in April 2004 cut all funding for women's centres. Why? According to the premier, they didn't provide a service. When other provinces have also watered down their women's policy roles, eliminated them or neglected to introduce them, the voice of women in the policy of provincial matters is silenced. How very convenient. With no voice, perhaps some will come to believe the women's movement is dead, or maybe that we have really achieved equality and we just have not proclaimed it as of yet, so we can all breathe a sigh of relief.

We need to enlarge our scope of diversity and inclusivity to ensure we include disabled women, poor women. Only through enlarging our community of women will we find sustainability. Women need to collectively hold something for ransom (reproductive control springs almost immediately to mind) to shake out the apathy within the feminist movement and rally the troops.

The provincial ministries are confusing outcomes with activities. Women fear the government because of its potential. We see that levels of governmental controls make their insidious way into unchallenged regulation. If agencies decide to take the government money available and hold our breath every new fiscal year and government change, the best thing we can advocate for is a shift in thinking within the government funding bodies such as Community and Social Services and the Attorney General.

Never kid yourself. The governments have tons of money and spend it on the things they deem appropriate at the time. Near an election, they may espouse social issues, but often they do not. While they are busy ensuring they have expense accounts, the following tactics are being used to cut funding to women's programs.

A group of executive directors of northern shelters were gathered together and informed by their ministry representative that they needed to look at cost-saving measures. These women engaged in discussions about cutting beds and which agencies should be affected. Many of these women believed that if they came forward and volunteered to assist in these "cost savings" tasks, they would be in favour with the government and receive favourable treatment in return. The ministry rep coached them along the development of what he termed a plan, took it away, wrote it up and framed it as an agency self-created plan. Then he called another meeting to discuss how this voluntary plan would be enforced, and before long, funding was cut across this sector, with many agencies losing funding and seemingly having no one to blame but themselves. Pitting women's services against one another for meagre funding is a long-time favourite tactic of provincial governments. If we slug it out internally, our own survival will be threatened. If we help to destroy one another, it sure makes less work for the ministry.

The qualifications for ministry reps should be designed by women in the field, and the person hired should be someone from the field who is now disconnected from any specific organization. Ministry reps should take a more active role (operating within an approach such as that developed by John Carver) in the accountability of the agency, specifically the board and management, creating mechanisms and tools by which standards and ethics ensure that agencies are being run the best way they can be. Such supervision would decrease the power imbalance between staff and board.

Destroying Ourselves by Creating Alliances

I am looking at an auditor's report for the Ministry of Community and Social Services-funded violence-against-women agencies, and what initially strikes me is that page one states how much money the ministry allocated to these programs during the previous fiscal year. I feel like I am on a first date and my escort is trying to impress me straight away by telling me how much he made the previous year.

The audit's objectives are stated as follows:

- monitor the services provided by the transfer payment agencies to assess whether or not they are meeting the Ministry's expectation
- ensure that payments to transfer payment agencies are reasonable and adequately controlled. (Ontario Auditor's Report 2001)

Why is my back instantly up? Perhaps because there is no mention that the crimes of femicide and battering and sexual subjugation of females in our society have not been curbed. Perhaps because it feels as though the issue is about money, not people's lives. I know that this is a "financial" review, but archetypes run deep, and big brother is obviously here to breathe down the necks of women to ensure there is no mishandling of funds, while it strangely wanders away from the crux of the spending itself. Further, there is no mention of accountability to women.

The auditor's report from a content perspective is extremely accurate: there is insufficient funding to meet the demand for service. It cites examples of women and children being turned away due to lack of space; refers to homeless shelters (rather than abuse-specific shelters), which would potentially be unsafe and inappropriate in their lack of counselling services. It cites lengthy waiting lists for counselling and the need for the Ministry to ensure that service standards are "acceptable." This 2001 auditor's report also concluded that the "Ministry's policies and procedures were not adequate to ensure that transfer payment agencies providing services under the VAW program were reasonable and adequately controlled." What an ambiguous quote for misogynistic reporters to get hold of. What the report goes on to explain is that there is significant variance in funding and costs between shelters, a phenomenon explained by government funding allocations and is nothing to do with the performance of individual shelters. In fact, many of the suggestions with regard to governance and accountability were addressed years before in another report from the auditor, but have never been implemented. As far back as 1994, the auditor recommended the Ministry develop standards for service-qualifying areas such as definitions of core services, minimum staffing levels, acceptable waiting times, physical security and admission criteria. What the auditor's report of 2001 found was that the Ministry had not developed any standards for services provided under the VAW program.

The ministry's approach to accountability is restricted primarily to paperwork. Core services are to be reflected on yearly budget submissions, which include service descriptions and vague general information, and the loose use of the word "review," which terminology, unless you get your hands dirty and have the right people actually doing the reviewing, makes this document pretty useless.

Women who are experts in this field with an investment in the continued well being of anti-violence agencies need to be the ones who are the leads in any review, development of standards and accountability frameworks. Anything else is tantamount to letting a lawyer perform a lobotomy.

Here's a solution. Women who are "experts" within the anti-violence movement must be employed to ascertain service standards. With respect to accountability and governance, this 2001 report found that the Ministry had not ensured that

> agency management and the board of directors collectively had the necessary expertise and experience to discharge their responsibilities effectively; had not ensured that operating policies and procedures were adequate to ensure that service delivery was achieved economically, efficiently and effectively and had not ensured that internal governance and reporting structures for both financial and service information were appropriate. (Ontario Auditor's Report 2001: section 3.05)

The report points out that because transfer payment agencies are independently governed, these programs are not required to follow administrative policies and procedures prescribed by the same Ministry that funds them.

Whenever there has been any allegation of financial mismanagement within a shelter or rape crisis centre, the media is quick to jump all over it, ready to tear apart such services — part of a misogynistic attempt to cloud the real issue of femicide. What the reality of women's services has been is that in the evolution from voluntary feminist endeavour to large non-profit organizational structure, the funders — the ministries that are directly accountable to taxpayers — have neglected to offer guidance, structure, training or assistance that is of real value.

When women's agencies are funded out of embarrassment, guilt and tokenism, what is left out is actual investment. The money allocated to VAW initiatives was meant to signify commitment and investment in preventing wife battering and rape, but because money has been the only thing provided, what has happened is the absent-father syndrome: I have no time to spend with my children, nurturing and raising them; instead I'll send a healthy cheque each month, and my conscience will be clear and I'll be the hero. With women's organizations, that nurturing should have taken the form of quality training for management and boards, ongoing systems of assistance and accountability, mentoring and the inclusion into a responsive system of ministry governance, which would have assisted in the development of a whole new field of business.

Agencies have been slow to develop policy and procedure internally because they have never had to do so. With most organizations, policy development arises initially out of crisis. But when crisis is the stuff that fills up all the time in your day, there is little left over to work on developing these sorts of business skills. Reactionary policy creation is ineffective. Additionally, there seems to be a sense of shame about the concept of business and governance skills, as though the patriarchal system that oppresses us would rub off somehow and dirty the "real work" of women's shelters.

Beware the Buzz Word "Sustainability": In a memorandum from one ministry, the ministry representative encouraged that funding and grant proposals be submitted to a lottery-funded foundation and that models of sustainability be put forward in the applications. What does this really mean? We are going cut your funding sooner or later; we are just preparing you for the inevitable.

We need to create alliances with other agencies. The movement towards community partnerships is not a bad thing in and of itself, as long as the integrity of the agency and its philosophy can be maintained and not watered down or excuses made for it. Strategic collaboration should include clarity of purpose; congruence of mission; creation of value; communication between partners; continual learning and commitment to the partnership. It would serve our agencies well to examine all possible alliances carefully prior to engaging.

Stand by your staff and they will stand by the agency. Never shame anyone publicly. We are building respect and community. Stand by your philosophy. Feminism is easily diminished by organizational fear.

When Business Is Business

Whether or not it seems incongruous to our mission, anti-violence agencies are businesses. I think that notion alone starts to mess things up.

With the evolution to government-funded agencies and charitable donor status comes the inevitable financial accountability piece. The crossroads of women's services lie in several places, but none so critical as the moment of acceptance to a funding formula. Pioneers of the shelter movement rightly saw the key to sustainability was through financial security (such is the same old story of the experience of women in society), and to attain that money, we sold ourselves a bit for it. Certain realities exist: in order to provide a shelter service of any sort, there is a requirement of a physical structure, food, heat, light and basic toiletries. These costs were there even prior to shelters "professionalizing." The good women who sheltered the battered in their basements could only do so for so long, and the move to an independent location necessitated the money to pay the rent. But in the leap from basement to boardroom, several things have happened that are a direct result of the insidiousness of money:

- We had to control it.
- Once we had it, we wanted more.
- Once we had it, we needed more.
- We invited corruption.
- We shifted our focus off clients and staff and onto policy and procedure. Don't let anyone baffle you and tell you that personnel policy is created on behalf of staff. It is all about how to control staff, to keep them in line.
- We began to empire-build.
- Women in crisis do not need a hot tub. They need some money for food and a bit of dignity. I have witnessed petty financial controls over poor women by executive directors who boast shelters with better "amenities."
- Money gave us power over the women. "Can I please have $3 for smokes?" A shelter I know of has spent thousands of dollars showcasing the efforts of its agency and the personality of the executive director to world stages focused on peace-building. The executive director went to other countries and ensured her name appeared in the who's who of Canadian business. Meanwhile, front-line workers are prevented them giving women a personal needs allowance — a few dollars a day to sustain their feeling of independence and empowerment. Staff were directed to send women on the local bus, a terribly inefficient transportation system, rather than dare use a cab for any appointment.
- Money gave us power over staff. With staff financially compensated

for their work, they are subservient to the agency for that money to sustain them. Everything automatically now becomes conditions to your sustainability, and employers consciously or not have leverage to enact disciplinary measures, internal competition, invitations to curry favour and the sentiment that you are damn lucky to have a job at all.

- We invited unionization. There should exist no reason to impose another framework that embraces male power structures within a feminist organization if the organization does not embrace internal power-over dynamics. Unionization generally occurs when management starts an unhealthy pattern of secrecy. Communication is often poor within unions and the same dynamics are created between union stewards and the collective as exists between the staff and management.

Of all persons having positions within the agency, the business manager needs to have the humility to pay attention to, hear and work on her innate power. If she is unwilling or cannot resolve that she has any, you need a new business manager. Her role should be confined to business/financial manager and her job tasks very specific. She should not have any additional roles, such as a human resources manager. Holding the money card, she cannot play the dual roles with any degree of effectiveness. She should not have direct access to the board unless there is an equitable structure of representation within the agency, including all managers, and staff representatives. Otherwise, the imbalance of power and information and direct ear and linkage to the executive director will further create an unhealthy power dynamic.

The relationship between the board and the business manager and the rest of the management structure that sets budgets needs to be one in which the board is proactive in its vision, not reactive (scrutinizing budgets and then voting to approve or not). Being reactive sets the stage for friction between the budget creator and the approvers. The board, then, or the financial subcommittee, needs to budget to meet the vision instead of engaging in incremental budgeting. There needs to exist a policy on budgeting that stipulates that money is allocated to achieve the ends.

The business manager cannot be a peer of other managers such as program managers. She cannot have the ability to veto, alter or override any financial or budgeting decisions made by these other managers. Beyond budgets, there needs to be a financial plan for the agency, not merely a fundraising plan.

Control over finances, paycheques and the bank accounts, coupled with access to board meetings and privileged information that other managers may not be privy to, creates a structural power imbalance within the management structure (if there are other "middle management" positions) and within the agency structure. This structural imbalance, inherent in the financial function historically equated with patriarchy and oppression, when married with the access to privileged information, sets the stage for conflict at several levels.

One is the distance from the real work. In my experience, few women in the role of financial manager had any background in feminist studies or social work, little life experience of oppression and a weak or non-existent framework of feminism. Further, these women were not being required to obtain any training in these areas. Their direct involvement with women and children was at arm's length, if at all, and many front-line staff sought to maintain that lack of contact. They felt that the business manager was incapable of understanding her position of privilege, both in society and within the agency, and that she dealt with the women in too bureaucratic a manner.

Since we are no longer a group of well-meaning women hiding scared women and kids in our basements, and since we do operate million-dollar programs, the view of violence-against-women work as a business needs to shift so that we do not feel so vulgar when we acknowledge that fact.

The primary factor keeping our organizations afloat, besides our determination, is money, and since the political climate is shifting onto safety as a perception of external, "foreign" threats rather than internal, "he lives in my house and sleeps in my bed" type threats, the need for women's organizations to be financially secure is paramount, as is the marriage of money and business "savvy." The business world is not an arena many of us have had much time in, and it is imperative that we learn it enough to keep our organizations in existence and to give ourselves enough breathing room to stand back, re-assess and design new models.

If government taxpayers' money (yes, yours too) is no longer available, and there are no matrons leaping forth from the woodwork, the key to survival obviously is creative fundraising. Corporations are often reluctant to fund or donate to agencies such as battered women's shelters or rape crisis centres because they do not wish to be seen as tied to that particular "cause." Unfortunately, giving money to work against violence against women and kids is still seen as catering to a special interest group. So how can we get our hands in the corporate pockets? Changing the perception of the "special interest group" is primary, and not necessarily on the larger social stage, but in how marketing is done and pitched to the big corporations. And the women who work in and run and who hold positions of power in the corporations need to make a moral stand. Get with your sisters, honey — even if you can afford to stay at the Howard Johnson's when your husband has beaten you.

We need to find ways to make money to sustain ourselves. We have got to get around the disgust of the corporate world long enough to make a buck to two at arm's length in order to be self-sustaining. Many non-profits now have a for-profit sub-program.

'We need to create shelter-specific internal systems of accountability. Consider the following points:

- Maintain your autonomy as a profession.
- A good system of accountability sets a set of ethical standards by which competence can be measured.
- Create impenetrable standards and ethics documents.
- Internal "investigations": Many women's organizations, when experiencing an internal crisis that appears to be beyond established conflict resolution guidelines, will employ a consultant to come in and perform an organizational review and conflict resolution with groups or individuals. Many of the consultants have little or no background in violence-against-women work, are poorly screened or are the result of board nepotism. Most of the women I spoke with felt these consultants, investigations and subsequent reports were utterly useless.
- Review programs.
- Evaluate programs.

When a system of accountability, or performance management, or service delivery evaluation is imposed on violence-against-women organizations, always remember to think through the hidden agendas. When financial, statistical and narrative reporting is not sufficient to pacify funders, could this review really be a tool to establish a lack of necessity or incompetence? Such imposed systems, which often take the form of surveys and written evaluation, are talked up as if they are truly client-focused. Anyone with a shred of understanding of the make-up of the client population knows how misguided this is.

CHAPTER 3

ORGANIZATIONAL ADMINISTRATION

INTRODUCTION

Why would a feminist agency not be the first in line to implement "family friendly" workplace initiatives? Given that the very movement was a driving lobby force behind many changes to women's experience of freedom and ability to work outside the home, for pay equity and employment standard changes, why are we so frantically trying to catch up to "family friendly" employers of the mainstream world?

- The money argument: "But we can't afford it": The good news is that employers are waking up to the fact that a happy, well-adjusted employee is one who sticks around. They're learning that employee retention is in their best interest: losing an employee costs anywhere from 1.5 to 2.5 times the exiting worker's salary to pay for replacement, orientation and training, according to many business expert.
- It's about respect. It's a recognition that the people who work for you have responsibilities beyond themselves. A family-friendly work environment is one where employees have the ability to fulfill all their responsibilities at home and at work without fear, guilt or anxiety. (Vermond 2004: 101)

Criteria for what makes an employer-friendly workplace include: on-site daycare; maternity leave top-up; flexible work options, including telecommuting and job-sharing; extended vacation allowance; extra personal days off; unpaid leaves of absence; adoption assistance and other personal benefits.

THE PHYSICAL ENVIRONMENT

Shelter-managing agencies need a beautiful environment, and clients need to take ownership of beautifying the environment. This in turn necessitates a good life-skills program. Staff need a beautiful environment in which to work in order to offset vicarious trauma. I have heard the stereotype of the dirty shelter, and many agencies have worked hard to combat the negative images of shelters in the community. However, shelters must be places of beauty, not just clean and safe. Women deserve so much more than that.

Too often there are no physical tools to aid in the work of counselling. The physical space is poor, lacking in privacy; there is no office conducive to effective listening. Staff need a physical space to which to retreat, where they are not accessible for a few minutes. The strain of constant accessibility on single-shifted front-line counsellors is enormous.

The reality of shelter work is the constant demand for the essential and the non-essential, with no chance to prioritize — you just get it all done. This comment does highlight several key issues: the resentment of those who "have it easier," which parallels the hierarchy of victimization phenomenon we see occurring, and the need to both acknowledge and alter the breakneck pace at which shelter workers are often required to perform their jobs.

> When I went to work at a rape crisis centre, I was struck by how my spirits collapsed the instant I walked in the door. At first I thought that the deadening atmosphere was the residue of the thousand acts of violation that had been recounted between those walls. But soon I saw that it was not the traumas themselves that were sucking oxygen out of the rooms, but the way in which we pursued the fight against them.
>
> The shabbiness was an aesthetic, an integral part of the culture... the insufficiency, the misery were almost beloved, for they underscored how much we had suffered, how pitiful were our resources in the face of the mighty opposition, and how good we were to volunteer our time in such conditions. Any attempt to lessen the physical sadness of the place was met with strong resistance as being somehow unfeminist, unworthy. (Wolf 1994: 152)

So if there exists the sentiment that the shelter/rape crisis centre cannot look like the Holiday Inn, why is it that there can exist within this culture the notion that the administration offices can? At one agency, the shelter and the administration are housed within the same building, the doors fronting onto the same street. The administration offices have professional cleaners come in, the newspaper delivered, take-out food delivered, new furniture ordered. The shelter does not. At another, the executive director provided herself with a huge expensive wood and glass desk and leather chairs. Counsellors in the same shelter used furniture that had not been replaced in years and was shabby and worn.

One of the number one issues for staff burnout is the workload. With the ability to work anytime, anywhere, with the "advancements" of laptops and cell phones and e-mail, why are we not ready to leap into the virtual office world? Sleep deprivation resulting from ridiculous scheduling is a liability, not only to the individual, but to the client's safety. Why is the schedule one of the most common areas of hotly contested negotiating?

THE EMOTIONAL ENVIRONMENT

Naomi Wolf talks about having three choices when working with the horrors of violence:

> One: We could protect ourselves and just do our jobs, thus delivering professional warmth to the survivor, but undergoing the internal detachment that so many medical workers describe. Though that option would have been efficient, it would have wreaked havoc with our self-image as compassionate, selfless fellow sufferers. Two: We could make a great leap of the heart and stretch of the imagination, seeing the hellfire clearly and yet admiring the strength of the survivors, so violated, yet so intent on healing. We could praise ourselves for fighting the good fight, and take pride in the inch by inch legal changes that we were bringing about. But that option would have required us to think very highly of ourselves and of other women, two achievements that do not come easily to women. Three: As the conventionally feminine culture of the centre led us to do, we could make female victim status into our main source of identity and even prestige. Thus, we could see our "enemies" as eternally evil, all men as potential rapists, sexual violence our unchangeable lot, and the painful nature of our work as proof that we were better than everyone else. This third option prevailed. (Wolf 1994: 156)

> Thoughts are just one part of our bodies' wisdom. A thought held long enough and repeated enough becomes a belief. The belief then becomes biology. Beliefs are energetic forces that create the physical basis for our individual lives and our health. If we don't work through our emotional distress, we set ourselves up for physical distress because of the biochemical effect that suppressed emotions have on our immune system and endocrine systems. In several scientific studies, "inescapable" stress has been associated with a distinct form of immunosuppression (suppression of the immune system response). (Northrup 1994: 35)

Shelter workers experience fibromyalgia and chronic fatigue, problems with bowels and stomach, migraines, and the obvious — depression and anxiety. There have been colon/bowel studies linking these ailments with sexual abuse survivors, and these are also seen as affecting those who are counselling survivors and experiencing vicarious effects (for example, see Brown and O'Brien 1998; Mitchell and Dyregrov 1996; Delongis, Folkman and Lazarus 1998; Schachter et al. 2004; Longstreth 1998).

There is no time built into our work for dialogue about the pain of this work, about effects of women's stories and experiences on us as counsellors and front-line workers. There needs to be an open statement that this burden exists for staff and debriefing mechanisms *must be* built in. Down time in between clients is too often consumed with administrative tasks, which there is really no time to complete due to huge client loads. It is necessary to have healing rituals for staff. We need to re-think the concept of "vacation" and explore alternatives for staff such as paid healing retreats.

While the agency can support the implementation of tools for self-care, as a responsible feminist person the onus lies upon us to follow through with self-care practice and to access resources offered to us. The responsibility of the agency, within the role of supervision, case management and staff meetings, is to offer staff a place to put their emotion into a larger context in order to keep people from becoming "stuck" in their emotion and to assist in transforming emotion into action. The management's role, then, is to provide the container in which to explore ways to further politicize, enact social action, advocate for change and re-contextualize staff's experience, which may a by-product of vicarious trauma. We must give the staff something useful and proactive to do with it.

> When we change ourselves inside by allowing ourselves to experience and own our long-suppressed emotions and woundings as well as our hopes and dreams for ourselves, our families, and our planet, the conditions of our lives change on the outside. Working for social changes must go hand in hand with the willingness to heal within ourselves all the internalized messages of blame, self-doubt, and self-hatred that are encoded in our very cells. Otherwise, our actions originate out of unhealthy places within us and often recreate polarization and pain. (Northrup 1994: 655)

All staff need to have some duty or job requirement that removes them from the nucleus of the agency and takes them outside into the community as a touchstone to reality and a balance from the insular world of the shelter, which has been structured to keep the community out. We must ensure job descriptions are broad enough to encompass this and that management actively solicit interests from staff and links them up with the opportunities for such external involvement.

> *The coming together is not necessary for the work, but for the spiritual fulfilment. We would do the work anyway, within the agency or not. The need is community to sustain us. — B*

Many agencies tend to steer away from coalitions and have discouraged or prevented staff from attending their meetings. This is a huge mistake. All employees benefit from participation in coalitions — for resource and information-sharing, contacts, strategic alliances and self-care through connection with those in the same roles.

The following guiding principles for peer support embrace a feminist framework:

- the need to continuously build community;
- freedom to define who we are as women;
- women holding women in regard without judgment;
- asking for help/receiving help when needed;
- rallying around one another when support is required;
- issues are not intrinsically personal, but team issues;
- commitment to ongoing communication;
- commitment to addressing vicarious trauma;
- creating touchstones to retain feminist framework;
- interjecting humour whenever possible; and
- team members have onus to engage those who are not participating or do not appear engaged.

Supporting these principles requires structures and frameworks, such as group meetings and supervisions, staff meetings and opportunities for interaction, days away, retreats and internal collective training, and a clear agency-supported rationale, supportive policies and referenced documentation.

If femicide is a war on women, then let women create the appropriate patriotic subculture that gives ghosts of murdered women voices and provides a historical contextual retelling to ensure the generations of women that follow will understand their role within the bigger picture. The key elements in patriotism are these: "Brainwashing" to gather support for your cause will assist with creating a climate that will feed the desire to maintain and create sustainability. Re-enacting and retelling women's "war" stories of forging this movement — successes and failures. This needs to entail not merely a recounting of the chronological history, not just a re-cap of the issues, but the detailed account of the birth of the feminist movement, the creation of anti-violence services, the lives of the individual women who shaped this movement, the women who lived, the women who died.

We need to find a mechanism, a creative mechanism, to celebrate the sub-culture, to push our reality to be the culture. We need feminist "war" movies, memorials, pop culture. Allow for the women of experience in this field to re-tell of their struggles, give them permission to reminisce. Juxtapose women workers with women clients without differentiation, just as the soldiers and the victims were one and the same, sharing the same collective experience, the same post-traumatic stress disorder.

Symbols, such as the sickle and hammer that symbolized communism, will infuse meaning. Women's organizations need communal symbols to call our own, to infuse violence-against-women work with an identity, regardless of agency. This will offer not only an advantage in fundraising but in the collective identity of anti-violence workers.

Much of this hypothesis links with the collective unconseious at least to the extent in which the playing out of killing our grandmothers of feminism occurs.

> The elder female is somebody we have always known. She is there in the corner of the female unconsciousness, quiet, fierce, loving, obliterating. She explains some of the impulses that agitate and confuse us. I've noticed that daughters are hard on their mothers, much harder than sons are. Women will romanticize their fathers and forgive them many sins and failings, but toward their mothers they show no mercy. Whatever the mother did, she could do no right. The mother was cold and negligent, the mother was overbearing and smothering, the mother was timid, the mother was a shrew. Even feminism did not cure us of our mother hatred, our mother flu. We cling to our anger at our mothers. We don't want to give it up. It protects us.

> At the same time, women remain quite close to their mothers…. Women need their mothers. They blame their mothers, they dream of killing their mothers, but they keep coming back for more mother time. They want something, even if they can't articulate the desire. (Angier 2000: 233)

As Natalie Angier explains in her book, *Woman: An Intimate Geography*, the structure of Western lives don't easily accommodate long-term links between older and younger women. We expect help from older women, and our mother is the only older woman we know. She points out that when women seek a therapist, they seek a woman who is older than they are. We are not looking for our mother figure, but in the senior therapist, we are looking for the missing elder.

Angier goes on to note that in the 1970s, when women talked about sisterhood they fell into the habit of "apartheid by age": young women bonded with young women; older women split off and formed their own groupings. Barriers between generations are codified by names such as "baby boomers," "Generation X," etc. We tend to make friends and acquaintances along our own chronological peers, "thus we end up with girlfriends who are in the same precarious place as we are, anxious for all the same reasons, and we keep looking for our mothers, and those mythical creatures our female mentors" (Angier 2000: 236). The problem is that a group of same-aged people is inherently unstable. "Peers will compete just as siblings compete" (236).

We need elders in this work. Even if our elders harboured a belief that we now find offensive, we need to integrate this experience and these pioneers as part of our learning, not disassociate ourselves and cut these women out of our collective experience.

COMMUNICATION SKILLS

I have read many wonderful books on women and their uniqueness. Much of our incredible strength and wisdom lies in our gender differences from men in the ways in which we learn, grow, comprehend, know, communicate and connect. The sad part is that there are few stages in the world as it has been created for us to maximize these skills and gifts. The mainstream workplace is a prime example.

When the memos start to fly, the end is near. The memo is used as a tool for the passive-aggressive, for the creation of "paper trails." The memo is not so benign a method of communication as it seems. Lack of trust and good faith are evident when memos are sent back and forth about petty issues: why is this dialogue happening on paper instead of in person? It is the experience of long-term staff that when many memos are sent, there is deep fear, mistrust and oppression. Women understand the power of language. It has been used to marginalize us, to co-opt our power and our experience. Therefore, when it comes to correspondence, yes, words do matter. I have been told that to discuss memos is picky and minor, but some of the stories relayed to me by front-line workers and middle management spoke of memos used as tools of oppression, containing threats, abusive language and inappropriate remarks and allegations.

The need to communicate in person is paramount. We find many barriers to having large participatory staff meetings and therefore become reliant upon communicating by e-mail, fax, voice mail and memos, to our detriment. Unless the content is utterly benign, communication needs to happen in person.

Policies have followed from direct service. Organizations developed to meet need; out of need flowed delivery of service, and out of delivery of service, we saw the need for standardization of procedure and the subsequent development of policy. This was a natural organic development of a new field of practice and new organizations. However, within many long-standing organizations, policy and procedure on various levels, from board governance to direct service, are often incomplete or in progress, so that no clear definitions exist. Many policies remain in draft form, and have not been reviewed by staff, management or board, and have not been approved. Nor is there any mechanism to ensure policy is reviewed annually or bi-annually.

The situation is further exacerbated by the nature of government funding. New programs and initiatives that are funded by the government virtually only allow dollars for the direct service costs of running the program. The funding envelope is often not inclusive of the need for office space for the individual to run the program, nor for development of policy and procedure to accompany this new program. And when there is no budget for something, it rarely happens. So the outcome is the program operates without policy to guide it, often for years.

The following are further problems with policy and procedure:
- Staff are not often not involved in creating policy. Many identify that they are not interested in policy development, but there is also no discussion about the value of good policy and no skill-building around creating policy. Policy can be developed in creative ways!
- There is no standard application of policies.
- Policy can evolve into use merely a disciplinary tool.
- Policy is too often created on the back of an individual or a particular incident. Reactionary policy is resented and ineffectual.

No one likes their time to be wasted in meetings. People want to feel heard, remain on topic, come prepared to address the topic and experience a willingness to participate. The woman facilitating needs to ensure respect. There needs to be humour and there needs to be food.

Perhaps the most common complaint among my interviewees, which spoke to both safety and productivity, was the use of non-verbal protest tools such as eye rolling, sighing and other uses of body language. When these factors go unaddressed, the meeting fails. Side conversations were a hot topic as well, from two points of view: those that viewed side conversations as a mechanism to gain support for personal agendas or to derail others, and those who viewed side conversations as an outcome of a silenced minority and the concomitant need to ensure diversity of voices. Side conversations seemed to signal the need to build in mechanisms of caucus and creative approaches to ensuring inclusion.

THE POLITICAL ENVIRONMENT
Power: The Terrible "P" Word

I have to recant, give up the old belief that I am powerless and because of it nothing I can do will ever hurt anyone. — Margaret Atwood

---

The segment on power could on go for the duration of the book, and indeed virtually every point made in this book could be linked somehow to this theme. So much of our difficulty is tied to the same old devaluing of women's work in society, that the traditional work of women — cooking, cleaning, child rearing — have no economic value, no impact on the Gross Domestic Product (GDP). We have ventured out into the world of capitalism and have strived to gain the same symbols of economic power as the men, while maintaining our "valueless" unpaid work. Those of us who have ventured into the paid work of anti-violence work are burdened with an instant conflict. While women's work is accorded no economic value, pollution, war, rape and assault do have a beneficial impact on the GDP. This is why there is no real effort to stop these events, to actually end violence. As women going to a paid position within the anti-violence field, we are actually contributing to the economic viability of rape and assault. We are making money off the backs of women by creating financial structures that feed the economic mill that is best served by perpetuating violence and offering token "solutions" and blood money handouts to women to keep us quiet about the lack of actual intervention in violence, and to keep us financially dependent on the violence continuing.

As long as patriarchs and feminists alike covet the notion that women are gentle, they will not look for the facts that dispute it. — Patricia Pearson

---

As long as we who are fighting oppression continue to play the game of competition with one another, all forms of oppression will continue to exist. — Anne Bishop

---

Agencies have undergone a debasement of feminism. This happened when women were forced, in order to secure funding, to impose a bureaucratic system of organization upon what began as a social change movement. The collective voice of women united in cause, the suffragettes, the early face of feminism, the bra burning, the marches, the quiet uprising, had to give way to cumbersome bureaucratic processes in order to satisfy those who doled out the money. The systems that were instituted mirrored those of the patriarchal world women had risen up against — the world of classism, sexism, old boys' clubs, inequality in the division of resources and power.

The organizing of women espousing feminism and equality was intended to give greater strength to the fight for social change. The many injustices named through grassroots political action formed the basis for an application for funding and demonstrated the obvious need. Violence, sexual abuse, sexism, inequality of wealth and resources were the identified social ills. Structures like battered women's shelters and rape crisis centres were the by-product both of a glaring social evil and of the guilt of those who had remained apathetic. After centuries of rape and oppression, women received some meagre funds and were expected to fix things.

Despite social action's role in birthing mainstream women's services, many organizations do not openly or actively engage in political action. They do not belong to lobby groups, social justice groups or coalitions. Employees who express an interest in being involved in such activities and groups are often blocked from attending. They are passively blocked by requesting that lobbying and political action be done on their own time. They are not compensated for time spent attending meetings, marches or other action. They are actively blocked by not being allowed to leave their scheduled shift to attend. Social action is also discouraged when the agency does not prioritize it.

Many staff themselves are apathetic towards engaging in social action and the turn-out to marches such as International Women's Day and Take Back the Night comprises as little as 2 percent of all employees. Should the organization not simply organize such events, but also expect that all staff attend them? Should that same organization not view involvement as work and appropriately compensate women for their attendance?

Many organizations do not have a mission statement that includes political action. I have found that frequently these are the same agencies that shudder at the term "feminism" and hide beneath benign language such as "family violence" and "domestic abuse." Somehow, the statements of beliefs have managed to state that they provide services for women who are abused, yet they are not politically active. That seems to me like opening a shop, serving food and charging patrons for it, yet refusing to acknowledge that it is a restaurant. Without a basis of understanding of the social and historical causes of violence against women, you are not capable of providing appropriate, ethical or quality services to those women who have been victimized.

Perhaps the most important aspect of anti-violence work is our ethical responsibility for social change. If our work is not grounded in this belief, then all the Band-aid provisions of service are futile. The goal of anti-violence work, the big one, is to work towards the elimination of a need for our service; to do ourselves out of a job.

Our continued funding is contingent upon the perpetuation of women's violation, abuse and murder. It is blood money, essentially, from a society that condones violence against women and offers up token dollars to house and counsel those victims. The tokenism of this funding is demonstrated by its woeful inadequacy. It forces women to beg predominantly male governments for enough to get by.

Interestingly, when lobby groups ask for nominal annual fees to be paid by member agencies, we see the scepticism about the value of their work, the selfish hoarding of the little we do have, and the questioning whether anyone should attend annual meetings because of cost.

When governments reluctantly throw minimal dollars into services and expect maximum bang for their buck, the pinch is felt. When agencies with similar purposes are forced to compete with one another for the same small pool of money, it is reminiscent of a lion's den and one poor lost deer. And in the fray, while we crawl over each other to secure our own futures, those that toss the funds our way can sit back and witness us tearing each other down and doing their job for them. Could there be any easier way to silence this "special interest group" (which makes up 52 percent of the voting majority). The situation of too few resources creates a heinous competition, and competition is a trait that has been socialized into women to oppress them since the dawn of patriarchy: if we are too busy in competition, we cannot organize and therefore will never overthrow.

In order to remain open and provide services, our reliance upon government funding is complete. Oddly, there are few individuals willing to privately fund such services (women, where are our matrons?). Since the funding flows from the government, political action against that very government is often discouraged or blocked by the administrators of both the funders and the receiving agencies And so, women are prevented from lobbying against government actions or endorsements that negatively affect the lives of the women we advocate for.

Examples of such cuts are cuts in welfare, failure to act on inquest recommendations, divorce law changes, child welfare reform, inappropriate criminal sentencing and immigration law. These far-reaching, insidious, provincial or federal decisions or actions make up the barriers and systemic abuses long ago identified by feminists as umbrella structures that perpetuate violence against individual women. The analysis of power imbalance and abuse within social systems forms the basis of feminist analysis. And should it not be expected that employees rally for the right of women and children to receive support and adequate assistance from the government?

But barriers to social action are also created internally, within the same organizations that rely on social change to stop the victimization of their clients. In all shelters and rape crisis centres, mission statements or statements of principles state that one of the core services provided to the women and children they serve is advocacy. Check it out, I am sure it is there, even advertised in pamphlets and other literature that promotes the service. Yet an inordinate number of these same agencies prevent their own staff from engaging in social action or participating in other organizations that are trying to affect social change. It is a glaring and odious contradiction.

If all employees of a women's/feminist agency do not at some time engage in political action as an aspect of their work, not to mention as women who have apparently espoused the cause, then they are not fulfilling the basic mandate of advocacy. Advocacy for women is not simply making a telephone call on behalf of a client to try and get them on a waiting list. Advocacy is intended to embrace the commitment of creating an equitable, anti-oppressive environment. This must fundamentally mean an understanding of the bigger picture.

It should be the agency's responsibility to insist that active participation in any form of political and social change action be a requirement and condition of employment. This should be imbedded within the job descriptions, offers of employment, ethical duties and obligations of service. It should be clear that a worker is expected to seek multiple avenues for effecting change. This could include lobbying for legislative action, public education, identifying and advocating for the elimination of discrimination, equal access and distribution of resources and opportunities. It is intrinsic in anti-violence work: we shall, we must, promote social change.

It is imperative to understand that violence against women is a tactic, that it is linked integrally to greater structures — social, political, economic — and that without change to these systems, equality cannot be advanced

> The intensity of the relationship itself may contribute less to stress than may the artifices of bureaucracy that are imposed to maintain imbalances in power and divisiveness. Since separation and autonomy are valued over inclusion and mutual support, both the workers and clients remain steeped in their mutual powerlessness; the barrier of professionalism that separates them remains firmly in place. (Finn 1990: 62)

Not only is social action a fundamental personal requirement of staff, it must be incorporated into the service we provide to women. There must be an integration of social issues within direct service practice. It is our obligation to involve the women, the "victims" themselves, in a global understanding of woman abuse. It is not enough to provide information of the cycle of violence, the honeymoon stage, safety plans and all the jargon created for service provision. Without contextualizing woman abuse within the structures and systems that perpetuate the violence against them, we participate in creating a horrifying class structure. If we as service providers are not engaging our clients in regular discussion of systemic abuse, we are breaking our own ethical responsibility for ensuring an equal distribution of resources — information, education — powerful tools, indispensable resources. Many statements of beliefs include the right of women to make informed choices. We then, as service providers, have the obligation to inform and educate.

Through an educational journey of our own, we became enlightened enough to feel we could assist other women in freeing themselves from victimization. So why are we not sharing our knowledge? Do we think these women cannot handle it? I have heard the argument that since these women have fled such traumatic situations, such debate would further add to their load, that it would be too much for a woman whose focus now is to secure housing, obtain custody of children and deal with their abuse. When did we become the ones to decide what a woman needs? To ascertain what information she can manage and just how much we should tell her? Is this not the image of the controller, the same imbalance of power she just left? Is there an assumption that workers should not discuss these social justice issues with clients because they will not comprehend? After all, many of us went to school to learn this. The underlying message then is that the client is stupid or at the very least less intelligent than we are as professionals.

This is not to say that workers should not have a level of expertise in the field of violence against women, but we must also give respect to experience and the vast knowledge our clients possess. Our clients, after all, have been living as women in this society, have left situations of abuse within their homes. If anyone has spent time reflecting on violence and the hows and whys, it is these women. Have a good social justice discussion and listen really well. You might learn something.

What I have found, sadly, is that shelter workers and rape crisis centre counsellors do not engage clients in frank political discussion because they themselves do not have the knowledge base to draw from. They do not know their stuff. It begs the questions, how were they hired and why is no one ensuring they receive the necessary skills and education to effectively perform their job? But often the problem is the face most frequently in the forefront: the boss.

Yes, the executive director is the one whose face generally graces the newspapers and appears in interview segments on television. And many of them know their stuff and have made a cognitive evolution to take on that role: they are strong leaders. We need more of them. The agencies they represent should be naturally strong agencies. These women understand the frameworks; likely from both personal and professional vantage points. They have lived oppression and actively work now not to repeat it within their own four walls.

Then there are the rest. Take a close look at the agencies that spit out executive directors and management like coffee from a Tim Horton's. How many have any background in violence against women work or even have a remote comprehension of the work of women's services? I have seen many come and go and leave destruction in their wake. They hark from unrelated fields. They do not use the term "feminism" and are not clear on what it means. They are classist, from privileged lives and white backgrounds. They are homophobic and racist, and in a position to tell you what to do. I have heard traumatized women speak of management who are outright abusive — abuse of their power, verbal abuse, tantrums, throwing things, sexually harassing staff, cruelty to clients. The direction of an agency is flavoured from the top down. Decisions of hiring, training, expectations, minimum service standards, political and community activism, media relations, endorsements and internal policy guide the day-to-day experience of staff.

If it is acceptable for leadership to have no understanding of social issues, staff will also be weak in this field. It is not part of the work climate. It is not an expectation. Of course there might be the token woman who is passionate about such matters and brings as much as she can to the rest, but as a whole, staff will be unaware and decidedly uncomfortable about speaking to social justice issues. Staff therefore cannot communicate with clients on these topics.

There is also a need for integration of social action into direct counselling work with children. Without it, we create the dependency we loathe in psychiatry. Here's a solution: politicize young girls. Get them young and teach them well. Infiltrate schools; find the keen young minds who sense they are missing out on the biggest peeve of their education. Ensure women's organizations are set up to also be training and learning centres for these girls.

Keeping Women Poor
Countless reports state plainly that levels of funding are not adequate; yet women's organizations continue to remain woefully underfunded. The 2001 Ontario Auditor's Report was frank: "It is clear that the Ministry's current method of funding does not ensure appropriate and equitable funding for shelters that is linked to an assessed level of demand and to services provided in the respective communities." A coroner's report into the 1998 murder of an Ontario woman at the hands of her estranged husband recommended that the Ministry review its funding to shelters for abused women and their children. Another coroner's report, released only a couple years later investigating another brutal murder of a woman by her estranged husband, made virtually all the same recommendations as the 1998 report, including that those recommendations be put into action, and again calling the provincial government to task on the under-funding of services to abused women. There was no change in funding levels. Despite these reports, an average of fifty women are murdered each year in the province of Ontario by their intimate partners. Yet the provincial governments focus spending on "related" services such as policing and the judicial systems; systems that by all accounts from women continue to fail them and that are utilized by only a small percentage of abused women. Since nothing is done to assist with the prevention of femicide, murdered women become a statistical leverage to increase wages

and funding in sectors left to clean up afterwards.

Government funding has often come in the creation of "new" programs, without research and proper needs' assessments and without adequate funding for existing core services. Money targeted to these programs cannot be reallocated to areas of need at the discretion of internal management. This results in underused services, creative internal measures and funding overpayments.

All shelters should belong to provincial or federal lobby bodies. It should be a requirement, not a choice. These are bodies that, when effectively funded and run, will have a greater impact than individual agencies. These bodies must be funded by the individual agencies. Agencies must be involved with and committed to them, not just reap the rewards of their actions.

We must join with other organizations to help mobilize women to vote in municipal, provincial and deferral elections, to understand the platforms. Many organizations fear that they are not allowed to do such activities and don't, without realizing the distinction between partisan activities and electoral activities. How can we work on empowerment of women if we do not educate and involve women the system that governs them?

We need to broadening the victim-only mandate. Victim-only mandates mean that, in the case of lesbian battering relationships, service providers' main job becomes screening who is being victimized and tossing out the person who is being abusive. The agency is only being prepared to hear a certain kind of story of victimization. This practice seems to centre on the experiences of white middle-class women, ruling out the possibilities that certain women might access help, such as drug addicts or sex trade workers.

> Broadening the mandate to work with those who engage in abusive behaviour can teach us about the layerings of privilege and oppression and the limits of simplistic binaries. It helps push mainstream feminist organizations to look harder at issues of racism and classism.
>
> We have to stop and ask, whose voices and whose stories are heard when we talk about domestic violence? Whose stories are not heard? Who benefits from how we currently respond to heterosexual domestic violence and who might be left out of those responses? If we address those questions, then we look at some of the different contexts and different experiences of violence in heterosexual couples that I don't think we've talked about in enough detail. For example, there's still a tendency for most of the analysis and services to be focused on middle-class, white women. Service providers almost expect to hear a certain script from victims about how they should talk about their stories. Either women learn how to present

their story in that way or they might be denied services. For example, a poor woman with street experience who might have experienced a lot of violence in her life, who has fought back, who is feeling angry, might not be heard as a victim. (Fallding 2003: 20)

I am loath to use the term "holistic," as it has often been debased, especially within a feminist framework. I do not want to be misconstrued as "watering down" the approach taken to date towards violence against women; however, if women are not treated as whole packages, good, bad and ugly, the service is not helping them, as they have to keep parts hidden or be dishonest to themselves or to the agency in order to access service.

We need to broad the shelter service mandate. This is a sore topic for many when it comes to fighting over funding dollars and how many beds an agency is funded for. Historically, women's organizations have been funded to provide emergency shelter service, and although this is still a necessity, shelter is only accessed by a very small percentage of women who require anti-violence services. To address the diversity of need, services must find the flexibility to fund programs in a way that meets the needs of the women and not just arbitrarily fight to retain shelter bed *per diem* funding. To meet the needs of rural women, women who would never use shelter services or women with means who would stay elsewhere, community-based services are essential.

Women's organizations need mandates that are loose enough to allow for service flexibility; otherwise the mandate needs to be reworked to meet the changing service demands. How agencies fulfil the mandate is subjective. We need to allow for a natural evolution in what we do. For example, perhaps the effectiveness of Take Back the Night and December 6th vigils has reached the end of its limit. We must now recreate new ways to capture the imagination and enthusiasm of an Internet culture. Why the resistance to combining anti-violence services, as long as they are feminist-based and gender-specific, being cognizant that the drive here is not to empire build, but to sustain and best serve.

The Incredible Power of Powerlessness
We have been shying away from the realities of women's hostility and aggression.

> Regardless whether we assign it a positive or negative value, we tend to conceive of violence as a collection of assertive, public acts: fistfights, bar brawls, gun duels, the collision of soldiers on a field. Violence is the spectacle of teenaged boys beating one another up and mobsters blowing rivals away. It is physical; it is direct. (Pearson 1997: 11)

We cannot ignore stratification and power imbalances within our field. Now, more than ever, there is an increase in power imbalances among women, and perhaps is this nowhere better seen than within the violence-against-women field. If we are to continue in our work in an ethical manner, as feminists we must begin to address this increasing stratification among ourselves, as we continue to pitch our message of inequality with men.

> We are all products of our socialization as women; this is perhaps, paradoxically, supremely so for women workers, who have chosen a field which requires them to emphasize their emotional sensitivity to others and their care-giving abilities. Yet, beyond this, there are issues of power relations within women's groups, which, if ignored, can breed mendacity and obfuscation. (Butler and Wintram 1991: 74)

Sandra Butler and Claire Wintram (1991) discuss the danger of workers falling into the "false equality trap" and ignoring the stratifications of power and privilege that exist. This is no more evident than in the gap that widens when white VAW cultures have to face their own racism.

> In the expansion years of the early nineties, rape crisis centres and the OCRCC (Ontario Coalition of Rape Crisis Centres) alike experienced significant growing pains and much internal debate. This period saw the first challenges to the generally white, middle-class make-up of the sector, and the response from long-standing advocates who felt an ownership over the anti-rape movement was less than graceful. These issues, combined with successive economic recessions and a climate of backlash against equality rights, forced the Coalition and the sector as a whole to turn inwards. (Khosla 2003: 28)

Issues that feminist organizations must examine to address power imbalances encompass every facet of our structure, our composition and our processes. It is our work as feminists to be doing just this.

LANGUAGE: THE FORK AND SPOON
OF OPPRESSIVE BEHAVIOUR AND COP-OUTS

> A major concern among coalition members is the trend within government to refer to all issues of violence against women under the rubric of "domestic violence." This submerges issues of sexual violence and effectively drops them off the public agenda.... It does not encompass the increasingly urgent situation of women who are assaulted by other family members, acquaintances, co-workers, clients and people in positions of authority. (Khosla 2003: 17)

Women have struggled and stumbled over language as though it were the most insurmountable of all of our barriers. Often it really is just semantics, nothing more, but many would have us believe that clouded in language is a myriad of issues that often get in the way of the real work.

> *As staff, we would be reprimanded for using "inappropriate language," by managers or peers. Often the reprimands from peers felt sharper than the ones from management. They were telling me, you're not feminist enough, you will never get it, never be one of us. They had the culture laid out, and when I had the audacious stupidity to use the word "lady" instead of "woman," I felt a door shut to my inclusion. Christ, these "women" even gave the clients hell. I mean, really hell, gave these poor women shit for their use of language only days into their stay at the shelter after leaving a husband who beat the crap out of them. These staff lorded their ability to police their very words over these confused people, and when I tried to make a correlation between fear of the abusive husband and his control and some of their behaviours, life became so unbearable for me, I finally was worn down enough to quit. — a shelter worker*

I heard similar stories from other women. What these certain intolerant women never seemed to acknowledge was the superficiality of these "remedies." Changing language does have a place in ending misogyny, but their analysis was ill-placed, alienating potential allies, other women, other like-minded women, in order to make some sort of point. The second flaw to me seemed to be the grossly North American white privileged lens through which they saw merit in chastizing the use of politically incorrect language, such as the terms "ladies" and "chicks." I could not help but wonder, as women told me these stories, whether a young woman, poor and enslaved by culturally oppressive rituals, facing a clitorectomy, really cared whether she was called a lady or a woman. Their energy seemed so misused.

What can be useful is learning the language of those in power and being savvy enough to use these tools to our own advantage — to be heard, to facilitate change. Yet we must remain cognizant that we are using their tools to get by and never assimilate them.

We can help to change definitions and reclaim language; we can form a language army. We can reclaim the words that have been used to oppress and help save men from themselves by helping to change the definition of what is masculine.

Language is useful when co-opting power. It denotes who has the education, the privilege and the power. We speak so often without thinking about our use of language, our choice of words, and the message or meaning implicit or explicit in what we are saying.

I hear our business manager saying all the time: "I can't pay you for that unless I have the paperwork." She will explain, if pushed, that yes, the paperwork is apparently necessary to please the auditors, but all I hear is that she has the money and the power to give it out or refuse. It's not her money. What I hear is my father bitching about how much mom spent on groceries, which she paid for from the allowance he gave her, to which she was accountable to him every cent, or might be beaten. All I hear is the patriarchy. The financial control. The bullshit. — BJ

It is easy to clarify our intended meaning, but we often never have the chance to do so, or to enter into dialogue with those who need to discuss this.

Call It What It Is: Femicide

For me, this is the biggest issue that we must truly own and acknowledge, or it is impossible to do any actual political action. The systematic murder of women for the mere fact that they are women is *femicide*. Learn it. If you do not know it, shame on you. If you cannot espouse it, quit your job today, it is the right thing to do.

What do we do? And why can we not agree on what to call it? Many shelters are terrified to name it for what it is: violence against women. Woman abuse. That is what we are about. Those who feel the need to soften it and call it "domestic violence" or "family violence" have issues of their own.

There is a very great difference between using all the appropriate language and chastizing other women for being anti-feminist for using language that is not deemed politically correct and understanding the power of language, the meaning and origins of words, the power of literacy and education, and the play and reclaiming of words which have been used as tools of oppression against us. The latter is far less easy to grasp.

It takes little more than memory to garner a vocabulary free of all gender bias, oppressive, racist, slang, derogatory and foolish nuances. Once you have committed this to memory, it is far easier to break into the ranks of the feminist movement within anti-violence agencies as they have formed themselves as a sub-culture of false perfectionism when it pertains to language. The solution is to create a language culture. Language must circulate freely within the agency at all levels; managers need to use the language of staff.

If you cannot use the term "feminist," it is time for you to bow out gracefully. If you cannot use the term "feminist" without a ten-minute explanation filled with disclaimers, it is time for you to bow out gracefully. If you cannot use the term "feminist" in social conversation to describe where you work and what you do, you need to bow out gracefully.

During a supervision session I was instructed that my use of language had to change. I was no longer to refer to men (arising from a particular

instance) as a "nut," a "loose cannon," an "asshole" or any other nega-
tive derisive remark. I was reminded that all people have worth and I
needed to reflect that in my language use. This particular "gentleman"
beat and raped his wife. Sounds like an asshole to me. — JJ

Do we call ourselves counsellors or workers? For women who are supposedly not concerned with power, we are really hung up on what we call
ourselves. How much does this have to do with the hierarchy versus the
collective? Everything — when we are part of a hierarchical system that
bestows male value-based titles. It has everything to do with the legislation
of VAW work, the battle against the BSW.

> An expansion of personal propaganda has occurred at the expense
> of our own self-awareness and personal competence. Because of
> the mystique of professionalism, we are not allowed to be ourselves.
> There are many forces at work which perceive a rejection of the
> professional mould as heresy. Organizational culture is a profound
> illustration of this. (Butler and Wintram 1991: 173)

Why don't we create a legitimate new framework for accreditation
generated from inside our field, rather than having it imposed upon us? Or
perhaps we could spend the time deconstructing our roles and relationships
and arrive at a place where this concept ceases to matter much.

We do not "fight" for anything anymore. We cannot use words like
"aim" or "target" or "shoot." Advocating is the most passive of descriptive
words for what feminists need to be doing much more of. I find that the term
"advocating" is too often thrown around when what we should be saying is
that we did very little but need a handy hiding spot. When agencies have no
clear model for advocacy that synthesizes the counselling and administrative
internal models with the larger social justice and political action that needs
to be taking place, there is no external work outside the agency. There is no
framework for mentoring new staff. There is no platform with which to plan
and specifically focus energy to work towards larger solutions. What occurs is
apathy, a organizational sense that "we are doing all we can just counselling
and staying afloat financially." There is no plan of when and how to respond
to critical events, no plan for creating social disturbance.

We are remiss sometimes as women when we buy into the language used
to keep women down, when we use language to degrade and react just as
a man would. Beware the misuse of reclaiming language: oppression and
abuse is nothing more.

CHAPTER 4

FEMINIST ISSUES IN THE ORGANIZATION

HIERARCHY OF FEMINISTS

Any woman who is up off her ass is part of the women's movement.
— Gloria Steinem

Women have spent much time seeking to establish the differences between us. Perhaps this is the result of our desperate attempt to find a voice. We have articulated differences in race, sexual diversity, victimization and feminist theory and practice. We have been so quick to compartmentalize one another that we have lost the thread of building connection, which is integral to trust, healthy interaction and conflict resolution. The notion of standing together with one's sisters has fallen into a deep abyss of staking a claim on the greatest diversity. The end result is that diversity cannot be celebrated within the whole, since we have all retreated to our little boxes with the appropriate label and function.

We have created a disparity of perception within the broader feminist communities, external to the agencies themselves. We have created a hierarchical structure of expert feminists compared to the "dabblers." Too often we perpetuate this climate by devaluing our own expertise, not permitting ourselves or our peers to take on new challenges — often public or instructional challenges.

> We witness small cliques created of the experts, and we see them hire the same women over and over for projects and consulting work and the rest of us peon agency women help to draft the proposals which generate her salary which far exceeds our own and we keep her employed. In turn she picks her favourites and generates work for them rather than putting the opportunity to work out into the greater community and let women apply for it. I am sick of never having the chance to show what I know in another forum. There is no point in even applying. They'll just give it to her, she is the queen. — J

We need to make room for one another. We need to invite each other in. Referring to the Ontario Coalition of Rape Crisis Centres, Punam Khosla reflects:

> The long hiatus from a public role has made the Coalition into a less than formal meeting place, shaped by the personal relationships of long standing participants. This has been less than welcoming for newer members who experience it as a private club rather than an open organization. It has also undermined the good will and solidarity needed for pro-active Provincial coordination. (Khosla 2003: 29)

She goes on to say that this would be "easily remedied with the development of a fresh consensus and a renewed sense of purpose" (Khosla 2003: 29).

Behind a lot of crabby, frustrated women, there's a feminist dying to get out. So what about those "anti-feminists" — the ones who constantly are defending the men, blaming other women, blaming their mother, spewing out rhetoric about women abusing men? Those who seem to wilfully engage in all the stereotypes the rest of us rally against? The waif models? The women in *Playboy*? The women who stay at home, make babies and ask their husband for an allowance? Really, "'those'" women have become anyone who is not on "our" side, those we perceive as sadly lacking in feminist education, with heads in the sand, as living a life of denial and gender role bliss. Many of us carry about the elitist notion that if only we could reach these women, pull them away from their sheltered reality and show them all the ways their lives have been co-opted by patriarchy, then the light would shine, and we would have them on our team. Why can we not accept these women at face value and let them be? Do they deserve the wrath and vilification bestowed on them by the supposedly marginalized population? Well, sisters, we ain't so marginalized if we can lord power in the form of knowledge and a sense of higher consciousness over the same women we seek to empower. And do not say you do not do it. We all do. The insidious judgments we are eager to toss out are clouded in pity or a rescue attempt.

What I do believe is that having the privilege of social awareness allows us the ability to challenge or reframe the thinking of those women who view feminism as a dirty word, or who construct their sentences to begin "I'm not a feminist, but…" and permit them the space to dialogue with the open-mindedness we claim to possess. The construct of feminism can seem very narrow and unfriendly to some, especially those who do not fit into the highly marginalized groups or who have been spurned for not being "feminist enough." Feel sorry for the women who cannot see themselves as a feminist within the framework as it should be, for they may stand to lose something should they embrace it. If our premise is that women are equal to men, why are we not then equal to one another?

Within the socially aware group of women, there is still the risk that the diversity of thought or the belief system subscribed to will be viewed as the . wrong line. As the feminist movement evolved, different schools of thought were birthed, and we tried on and wore what seemed comfortable. Although this diversity of feminist theory and practice appeared to offer choices, it has created further division between women as women, who all belong to the same oppressed gender. Men are men. There are not a whole lot of subgroups of men-theory. They just are. This sure helps create that unified front. Meanwhile, women are fragmenting all over the place, caught up in didactic conversations about the subtleties and power differentials between the Women's Liberationist, the Socialist Feminist, the Lesbian Feminist, the plain old Feminist, or any other label accompanying any other framework. It is worth keeping in mind that the only thing all feminists have in common is that they are women. Working from that premise saves a lot of grief and endless caucuses at meetings.

Is being a feminist not challenging ourselves, our structures, our own hierarchies? We ask this question in job interviews even though no one can agree internally on a definition. In fact, is feminism not more about choice than conforming? The establishment of hierarchy based on awareness, degree of oppression or victimization is perhaps the most grotesque display of self delusion I have ever seen. I have witnessed it time and again, the use of powerlessness to gain power. And no one seems to call anyone on it.

Solutions

> Many of the women attending Coalition meetings were founders of local centres, and have seen the sector evolve through its changes and expansions. As they prepare to retire or move on to other endeavours, new women from diverse communities and the younger generation are increasingly taking on the work. (Khosla 2003: 28)

"From time immemorial, the healer has achieved a place in society by means of special knowledge, training, and skills not ordinarily available to other members of society" (Miller 1991: 243). The elders in the violence-against-women field have incredible knowledge to pass on. We need to create a structure for this to occur, not only within our individual agencies, in the form of internal training and succession planning, but within the greater field. VAW elders need to create ongoing lectures and similar forums to share their herstory with a keen new generation. Most of the elders of the VAW sector entered this field via personal experience transformed into counsellor. Those "who recover most successfully are those who discover some meaning in their experience that transcends the limits of personal tragedy," commonly found "by joining with others in social action" (Herman 1992: 73). Let's allow them to tell of their journey.

The definitional ceremony metaphor structures the therapeutic arena as a context for the rich description of people's lives, identities and relationships. The rituals are acknowledging of and "regarding" of people's lives, in contrast to many of the common rituals of modern culture that are judging of and "degrading" of lives (Myerhoff 1982). What an incredible opportunity for women to tell or perform the stories of their lives before an audience of "outsider witnesses," who, borrowing on the work of cultural anthropologist Barbara Myerhoff, would then respond with retellings of certain aspects of what has been heard and who would shape specific traditions of acknowledgement. This process creates a lineage of herstory and a powerful sense of culture.

We must re-invent ourselves as a teaching facility to the community. Many agencies already provide education within schools on bullying and dating violence and public education to the community through forums, events and in-service trainings. The need to educate young women and men has never been more glaring nor the door more open. We need to create a culture, not a subculture.

Whatever Happened to the Radical Feminist?

Radical feminists can be identified by the way they get cynical when they're not drunk and get optimistic when they are. — Constance Leoff

The word "radical" is derived from "radius," meaning "at the root of things." We need to get back to being radical. Worried about making nice with other agencies? When the day is over, they do not really care. Worried about making nice with politicians? Come on, annoy some people. Feminism was described by United States evangelist Pat Robertson as "A socialist, anti-family political movement that encourages women to leave their husbands, kill their children, practice witchcraft, destroy capitalism and become lesbians." Doesn't that sound fun?

Think through why anti-violence activists are not readily engaged in law, politics and policy development. An astute article in a feminist magazine discussed the investigation of more than fifty missing prostitutes from Vancouver's downtown eastside and the discovery of bodies of some of the missing women at a pig farm. Suzanne Jay explored how the authority over whether the police investigation had been satisfactory was bestowed on the families, creating a privatized accountability. Accountability to the public, a valuable aspect of this "public" being the anti-violence activists in the Vancouver community, has been rejected. Her point is that engaging the feminists would mean a further police accounting of how raped and prostituted women are treated by police and the ineffectual history of police intervention. "Anti-violence feminists have an agenda of making the state accountable to the public and our agenda is political: women's rights" (Jay 2002: 8).

Anti-violence advocates in Ontario attended endless days of coroners' inquests into the deaths of two women, the inquests a few years apart. They attended unpaid, fought for their representation, witnessed their recommendations being wholeheartedly adopted by the jury, published in the reports and not acted upon. Feminists need radicals and advocates and persistence to avoid losing voice altogether in political and social policy. Where do you find the radical feminists? Women gathering in small groups, book clubs, cooking clubs, play groups and church groups. Let's each join one group in our communities and infiltrate.

The ability for violence-against-women services to create programs that respond to rapidly changing demographics has been hampered by a lack of funding, which leaves many marginalized women (woman of colour, sex trade workers, rural women, etc.) without supports. There has been a move to victim's rights over women's rights. This trend further places emphasis on the need to label the violence for what it is: violence against women. A reflection of the way the winds blow politically is the move to funding gender-neutral services and broaden the term "victim," "by prioritising these generic programs over locally based women's services and ignoring the reality that the majority of victims are women who have been subject to some form of gender based violence" (Khosla 2003: 15). For example, in 2000, amidst a huge number of murders of women by their intimate partners, the Attorney General announced huge funding increases for gender-neutral, law-and-order type services, entirely disregarding the obvious femicide, the gender-targeted "wave" of violence. Women are only given the media spotlight if they are dead or if they have lied. The focus of public interest has shifted to the perpetrator, not the victim.

We have witnessed a change in the child welfare field over the past twenty years, from arguing with the Children's Aid Society (CAS) that abuse towards the mother will actually harm the child, to arguing that being a child of an abused woman who is struggling to make changes does not warrant apprehension. In the anti-violence field, the CAS is part of our darkness — we have made them our enemy. If all you do is cry, then I have to carry all the joy in the relationship. When CAS apprehends, then we have to carry all the protection. Our struggles with child protection issues tap into our conceptions of motherhood, of our reproductive rights, of our privacy and dignity. Boiling it down, our struggles are about CAS versus VAW — who is the better mother?

OUR FEAR AND APATHY

My work is to be good company, to allow them to lean for a while on my unshakeable belief in their inner fire. Even on the good days, I can do more then this. Then, slowly, in their own time, their bodies open up, they begin to feel and taste the possibility of this wholeness for themselves. This fundamental goodness always awaits for us to discover it, if we will only gather together patiently and listen. — E-mail

British biologist Rupert Sheldrake posits that "all knowledge of the earth's past exists all around us as electromagnetic fields of information, or 'morphogenic fields'" (Northrup 1994: 646). Woman globally are speaking out and finding the courage to break through the collective morphogenic field of shame, fear and pain.... Breaking the silence takes courage. I know of no woman who has tapped her inner source of power without going through an almost palpable veil of fear, often feeling as though her very life would be threatened by telling the truth. Millions of women healers and wise women, and the men who have supported them, have been killed for telling the truth. It is little wonder, given the collective history of women, that we are afraid.

Beyond the integration of your own singular experience into the physicality of your body, lies the belief of cell memory. "Our bodies contain information that is beyond our intellectual mind's capacity to understand. We are much more than we think we are" (Northrup 1994: 646–47).

For a woman, coming off fear is like an addict coming off drugs.
— journalist Vivian Gornick

So many factors contributing to a climate that has become toxic; people suing, disgruntled ex-staff, union costs, ombudsman, human rights, these women are mad, want a piece of the pie, poor human resources and management, no pensions, afraid to buy staff out, forget this is a non-profit and the amount you can get is nominal anyway, looking for vindication. The primary reason why this occurs is a lack of leadership, a poor executive director.

Other factors women said topped their lists of reasons why the toxic environment is created and thus the fear, paranoia and distrust:

* lack of information
* colleague is fired
* no forum for open discussion and the fear of creating such a forum
* fear of the anger that may erupt should an open forum be planned; fear around the AGM and all staff meetings
* connections to others within the agency are sporadic and personality-

and locality-driven
- being too rule-bound encourages underground behaviours
- supports are needed also for the isolated roles of managers and executive directors to keep them grounded and less likely to incorporate destructive unconscious behaviours
- disparity does not tend to go over well in women's organizations (salary, power, access to info, treatment)
- linking mother issues with horizontal aggression
- no sense of the future
- the need to create a group identity, not just norms
- conflict resolution never starts with the conflict
- we do not acknowledge the level of intimacy we have with one another.

Solutions

Test invisible barriers: Management puts in barriers by telling you all the things you can't do and all the reasons why you can't. Do them anyway, see what happens. Test to see whether they are invisible barriers.

Find ways to invest in women's futures: Women working in this field deserve to be compensated adequately and to have pensions. We cannot permit women to retire to poverty.

Combat fear by sneaking joy and hope into the counselling relationship: Hope supports action. "Hope is always set in the context of time. It draws on the past, is experienced in the present, and is aimed at the future" (Duvall 2004).

We need to own our own dark, as Jungians would say. We do not tend to own our shadows, our embodied experiences of the fear, the negativity, from our past. We do not realize the damage it can do when we transfer the negative emotions we carry inside to the living world around us. We can build a new team, start fresh, and then it becomes someone's "job" to carry that darkness. It is not about her as a person; she is the one who is carrying it on behalf of the team; it belongs to all of them. Such was the frightening sentiment from many of my interviewees, that the potential for this to occur pre-existed and had little or nothing at all to do with job performance. It was a sense of wondering when would it be their turn to carry that "dark." Many felt that this occurred because there was no consistent conscious effort to build strong healthy teams.

Any sort of internal change further exacerbated the isolation, lack of transparency and secrecy experiences in the workplace. Investigations and internal reviews were handled abominably, with no shred of respect or dignity for those involved. As the dynamics played out, it became akin to warfare.

Management and all staff must understand complex group dynamics and see a role for themselves in affecting change. Often, anyone assuming the role of change agent is also given several more "hats" to wear in an effort to reduce their credibility and maintain the hierarchical structures that have prevailed and benefitted those in power positions. In *Feminist Groupwork*, Sandra Butler and Claire Wintram eloquently state:

> However much we feel weighted down by (male) polices and behaviour, the ability to carry on the struggle in such an environment gives us enormous determination. Each time we experience oppression, we dust ourselves down and deal with its stultifying effects. We become irritants for organizational change, systematically chipping away at patriarchy's foundations. Our outrage at organizational practices which further oppress women users of services provides us with the emotional strength to break out of the downward spiral of being a victim. Playing such a role in organizations reduces our manoeuvrability. We can use our personal power by exposing ourselves to the demands, sufferings and joys of women's group members. In doing so, we are likely to be attacked as acting "unprofessionally" or "unethically." For us, professionalism is expressed by the extent to which we can acknowledge how we feel and take responsibility for our actions. (Butler and Wintram 1991: 174)

Live the change you want to see. Often, it seems that change is merely rhetoric. In order to create meaningful change, those who desire change must live the change they want to see, must model the change for peers and management. In mainstream concepts of "coaching," this would be akin to "coaching upwards"; in effect, coaching your boss. In the violence-against-women sector, when we enter administrative roles, we fail to see that good coaching is good counselling. "Leaders" and administrators are quick to have answers when they need to be asking questions.

If you want to hear women's services deconstructed, go to a conference, training session, whatever, where a group of women's shelter workers are together in a room and listen. These women are more than eager to give their opinion, cite their complaints — they are in fact often boiling over to do just this. They will all let you know, quite bluntly, what they see as the flaws in the field, the injustices they experience within their own agencies.

When I undertook research for this book, I sought out many of the women with whom I had sat in rooms and partaken of animated evaluations. I sought out intelligent women, articulate women, those I knew had an opinion on this subject. Yet when I asked them to actually put pen to paper, send me an e-mail, I received peculiarly little feedback. Women said they would call. They did not. Women said they had a great deal to say and that they would send me responses to my questionnaires or e-mails. I would hear nothing. If I cornered one of these women in person, I would get some of the meat I was so desperately seeking. I took pages and pages of notes.

So why the fear of responding in writing? — confidentiality, job security, nothing changes anyway, no specific event sparked debate, apathy.

Apathy. There, I said it. Could it be that many shelter workers have lost their edge or never had it? Internally, we do not use our membership voting privileges in the non-profits we work in. We are often inactive in our unions. We blame management yet never attempt to use a management position ourselves to create change. Management is a tool, like any other, and if we despise the government in power, should we not get out there and vote, at the very least, if not run for office ourselves? The overthrowing of structures must begin within those very structures. They are far too established to topple them with mere complaints and dissatisfaction.

Maybe the condition of women is not as bad as it used to be, eh? After all, we got the right to vote. We own stuff, property even, and make a bit better money than we used to. Maybe we have forgotten. Maybe women who work in women's services are not the marginalized women. Perhaps we need to stand back and acknowledge that the mere fact that we are employed in an average-paying job that holds inherent power over victimized women makes us completely removed from the reality of what it means to be marginalized and oppressed. Most of us are white. Middle class. Heterosexual. Have status. Are not HIV. Are able-bodied.

Do we have any idea, really, of other women's experience? Anti-oppression training does not suddenly mean we "get it." Just because we went to a gay bar, does not mean we are not homophobic. It does not make us lesbian either. I watch violence-against-women workers take on the identity of the "oppressed of the day," espouse the trend most current and put on airs of understanding like a Halloween costume. If it is transgendered people, these women know one, in fact, they are friends with one, related to one, used to be one. They bandwagon political correctness, trying to be in vogue with the current marginalized group. These are workers who say and do "politically correct" things to maintain the illusion they feel accompanies their work, not because they have thought any of these things through.

And if we are the women with some power, however small it may be, do we not have a responsibility to use it on behalf of those other women, to better their experience? Is that not the very nature of our work? But how difficult is it to stand back and let another woman by? If I have something, a job with a decent paycheque, how tightly will I hold on to it? Will I give it up to another woman? A woman of colour? There are so few resources for all women that we greedily hang onto survival by guarding our own.

Staff will not come forward and make a complaint about another staff person in writing and stand behind it. More likely they will go to their manager and want them to fix it, but not take action themselves. This speaks to the lack of safety too and the ineffectual management. Have we come to a place where we are hoping to be rescued from our situation rather than facilitating change by standing up for ourselves and taking responsibility? Women of privilege can afford to be apathetic. This is a crucial reality that must be acknowledged in order to make progress in this community.

Ongoing "mini" crises keep us from getting to the bigger issues, which is a reflection structurally of the crisis we deal with, symbiosis of the abusive relationship. Destructive forces keep agencies adrift in the endless subtext of the "crisis of the day" and thus detract from the real work, the bigger picture, the grand social/political landscape in which our agencies operate. Boards and management must be astute enough to ensure this does not happen. If boards and management allow this to happen, or even encourage this by nurturing work environments that breed such crises (gossip, team dysfunction, unclear board roles, etc.) then there is another agenda at play. This is an agency that requires power and control by those who "lead" in order to exist. What will occur over time is a cancer of the soul within the agency and it will implode in order to try to recreate itself in the face of sickness.

The existence of post-traumatic stress is negated in violence-against-women work, although it is tossed about as a catch phrase when needed, much like the terms "feminist" and "closure." In VAW work, the post-traumatic stress may be worse than in other professions, such as police and fire-fighters, since the content of the work is a reality for all of us as women. We have all been victimized, or will be victimized, or have the potential to be victimized, regardless of any variables we may try to control. The subject matter, the felt experience, is close, too close, to home. Worse, VAW work has absolutely no glory:

- because women are the ones doing it;
- because society wants to deny the entire concept of violence against women and seeks to embrace gender neutrality, so essentially we are employees at a workplace that really does not exist;
- because there is no media embracing of the work, the job or the functions. The only coverage we receive is of basic service descriptions or when there is a strike or other service disruption, mismanagement or murder. There is no pop culture around VAW work, no movies, no cultural rhetoric. What the field really needs is a line of toy VAW-worker dress-up dolls, or a hit single;
- because ours is not thought of as a "real" job. It is not discussed at career day in schools;
- because everyone likes a good murdered woman story. What's all the fuss?

VAW work is not seen as an emergency service by anyone, including us. September 11, a decidedly horrific day in history, continues to define crisis culturally. The images of emergency workers, the heroes in our society, were once again mostly male heroes. VAW workers are not in the public perception of emergency workers.

When no money is put into VAW services, this clearly demonstrates the devaluing of the work. And, aside from the uniforms, there are some crucial differences in crisis trauma work:

- Fire fighters and police are not required or expected to form any bond or relationship with their clients; there is no expectation of client interaction. There is a new "wave" of policing wherein police are to be trained and sensitized to meet the needs of the clients and not further traumatize them. Ironically, we, the VAW workers, are the ones who are expected to provide them with the training they require.
- We are inherently closer to clients given our commonality of experience as women.
- The dark side of shelter work: the torture, ritual abuse, murder. Although police do see many horrific crimes, many of the women who seek VAW services do not regularly access police services. Therefore VAW workers are in ongoing contact with highly victimized women in a much more consistent and deeply profound way.

> *I remember being at the shelter for six months and a woman came to the door. She had just escaped a cult. They had just cut off her arm at the elbow. After that day, I was prepared for pretty much anything. — E*

And sadly, generally, these brutalized, marginalized women will not access shelters and mainstream services. We do not see the women in our society who really have it bad, and when we acknowledge that to ourselves, it is overwhelming. One solution is storytelling. Stories are not about the person, they are the person. Stories help us organize our experiences. They provide a rich description of experience. Allow for staff to tell their stories. Make room.

WOMEN AND COMPETITION

> Female primates are not good-girls, and they fight, and they're hierarchical and greedy, and they can be murderous toward each other. Nevertheless, the primate norm is a chronicle of female interdependence, of female solidarity; and here is where we differ from most of our primate cousins. (Angier 2000: 274)

Yet, historian Gerda Lerner notes that women appear to be ignorant of their history and reinvent the wheel over and over, the wheel being

> the awareness of women that they belong to a subordinate group; that they have suffered wrongs as a group; that their condition of subordination is not natural, but is societally determined; that they must join with other women to remedy these wrongs; and finally, that they must and can provide an alternate vision of societal organization in which women as well as men will enjoy autonomy and self-determination. (Lerner 1986: 12)

Lerner explores the creation of the institution of patriarchy along the historical framework of the evolution of societies from gathering and hunting to the domesticating animals and agriculture. The woman became wholly isolated and reliant therefore upon the only person close to her, her husband. Without the wandering of the gathering society, women were not self-reliant but developed dependency upon the male to meet their needs.

> With this gradual, complex, and revolutionary transformation from foraging to the fatherland, the worth of women to one another also changed, for much the poorer. The strategic sorority was swept aside. If there are no tubers to be dug or forests to rummage through, and if vast tracts of resources are held by men, what can a woman do for you? In the neo-human brain, a woman who is not your relative is a potential threat beyond anything seen elsewhere among primates. (Angier 2000: 282)

We are jealous of other women, We will not accept one woman doing better, being promoted, gaining wealth. We must bring her down. We cannot honour each other without resentment. Women tell stories of one another's inadequacies. Each of us needs to be the starlet; there is no room for more than one woman. Women are also worried about what other women think of them. We buy into the assumption pretty girls must be dumb; they cannot have the looks and the brains too. In fact, no one can be too anything and not fall under scrutiny. Too ugly, too pretty, too smart. Any deviation from baseline normal is questionable. Covert competition is insidious. It is a construct we need to actively struggle to free ourselves from.

Solutions
Mentoring girls. Demonstrate a lack of fear and competition by embracing young girls and introducing them to this field.
Accept apprenticeships. Let's permit ourselves to admit we can learn so much more and establish learning apprenticeships with other women within the field.

FEMINIST ISSUES IN THE ORGANIZATION

Let women bring what matters to them into the workplace — goddess, myth, their roots, native culture.

> If you are or ever have been a girl, you know that the first job
> of being a girl is learning to survive in a group of girls.
> — Nathalie Angier

Two girls play together very well. Three girls play together, and someone cries. This was so clear when we were little girls, at least to my mother, who witnessed my friend Lisa and I playing happily until another friend showed up, and sooner or later, someone's feelings were hurt. Two of the three would align themselves against the other, and terrible things were said, and the third was painfully left out in the cold.

> Girls in groups are — how shall we say it — what's that word that we persist in thinking has a meaning only for boys? Aggressive. Of course they are aggressive. They are alive aren't they? They are primates. They are social animals. So yes, girls may like to play with Barbie, but make the wrong move, sister, and ooh, ah, here's your own Dentist Barbie in the trash can, stripped, shorn, and with tooth marks on her boobs. (Angier 2000: 239)

Couple that with the primary desire of girls to want the attention and acceptance of other girls, not boys. No one wants to be the one left out. We work hard to keep alliances that enable us to be connected and secure. Studies of relational development of women note the centrality of connection and affiliation in women; this correlation to a woman's sense of self and how this experience of connectedness influences a woman's approach to conflict and confrontation. As soon as girls hone their verbal and social skills, at around ten or eleven, they become aggressors of a different kind. They abandon physical aggression for a more subtle, lethal sort.

> The fundamental mistake that feminism has made is to equate political
> weakness with moral innocence. — Patricia Pearson

> The problem with ignoring female aggression is that we who are aggressive, we girls and women and obligate primates, feel confused, as though something is missing in the equation, the interpretation of self and impulse. We're left to wander through the thickets of our profound ferocity, our roaring hungers and drives, and we're tossed in the playground to thrash it out among ourselves, girl to girl, knowing that we must prove ourselves and negotiate and strut

and calibrate but seeing little evidence of the struggle on screen or in books or on biology's docket. We are left feeling like "error variants," in the words of one female scientist, wondering why we aren't nicer than we are, and why we want so much, and why we can't sit still. (Angier 2000: 242)

We are taught that aggression in women is unacceptable, abnormal behaviour, and women who exhibit aggressive traits are demonized. Woman are socialized to avoid conflict; we have not had much practice at it, and generally not within our intimate relationships. Many women will tell you about their struggles over confronting their mothers and their partners. Women seek intimacy and connection within the workplace, and, therefore, peer and supervisory relationships must be viewed as intimate relationships, which changes the ability of women to confront.

An interesting model of relational group work proposes that establishing connection and intimacy is a necessary prerequisite for the surfacing of conflict or the challenge of authority. An excellent article by Linda Schiller (1995), "Stages of Development in Women's Groups: A Relational Model," looks at the differences in gender in therapeutic groups. Citing Hartung Hagen's research on all-women groups and conflict, Schiller notes that a high degree of trust and safety must have occurred for members to feel comfortable in allowing conflict to surface. What Schiller proposes is a relational model where members must first establish a sense of safety in their group affiliations and connections before they are able to challenge or confront one another. This group model also proposes that the stages of group development differ between men's and women's groups after the initial common stage of preaffiliation. The next stage in women's groups is to establish a relational base rather than a power and control stage, as seen in male groups. Following the importance of connection for women in their lives and in their healing process, the time spent in the second stage of group development is dedicated to establishing common ground with one another, and the facilitator, and seeking approval and connection from other group members and the facilitator. Schiller states that women are so frequently disempowered in their lives that a sense of safety in the world and therefore in a group is not something that can be taken for granted. This safety must be established as a prerequisite to greater intimacy and self-disclosure.

Despite the fact that Schiller's relational group model is based upon a "vulnerable" population, I feel it is applicable to all groups of women, and particularly VAW workers. All women can be seen as marginalized as a result of their gender experience; women working in the violence-against-women field are highly likely to have been survivors of violence personally;

the impact of working with traumatized women has a direct impact on the spiritual identity of the workers, who will embody the vulnerability of their clients.

Often at this developmental stage, women verbalize their fears and anxieties as they reach for safety and assurances that this experience will be different. If the woman is acknowledged in her experience and receives reassurances that the experience is a shared one, or someone else verbalizes what she too is feeling, this establishment of commonality, combined with a sense of security, leads to comfort and an ability to move to the next stage of group development.

How does this play out in the workplace? We are all seeking connection with other women. We often enter this work based on common experience with the violence against women. We seek a connection with like-minded women. What we do not do is spend time verbalizing the "me too's"; why not? There is a fear of the truth, a fear of being seen as a client and not as the professional, a fear of nakedness, boundaries of professionalism imposed upon our roles, the lack of a forum in which to do this as we are compartmentalized in our work or discouraged from "talking." It's seen as unproductive down time.

The third stage in group development is presented as "mutuality and interpersonal empathy." This stage corresponds with what has been known in group theory as the "work stage," the "ongoing phase" or the "intimacy stage." According to Schiller's relational model, this is the time when women's groups move past the establishment and recognition of the members' similarities and into a safe, sacred space of trust, disclosure and recognition and respect for differences among the members without sacrificing the thread of connection among them.

I will tell you right now — we virtually never get to this stage within the organized agency structure. We may get to this stage as staff sub-groups, but not as a staff team or agency. Those who jump ahead to this third stage and disclose without going through the stage of trust and connection risk many things. They may do so either as a result of their own issues (old behaviour, creating a lack of safety for themselves) or as a fault of the facilitator, who in this case would be an executive director, team leader, manager, peer mentor — the person who has not properly guided the group through the second stage. If the facilitator's basic philosophy is one that stresses mutuality not only between members but between members and the facilitator, and if she promotes group members helping other group members, then the group dynamics will more likely reflect her belief in the power of growth through connection.

The facilitator, in order to create the environment of empathetic attunement, must have an interest in, an investment in and a responsiveness to the subjective inner experiences of the others, the group members, combined with a mutual intersubjectivity. This correlation between group facilitator and executive director or manager plays out to require a therapeutic approach to team building and staff cohesiveness. The manner in which interpersonal connection is made must be constructed from the genuine shared philosophy in the approach to violence-against-women work, a respectful understanding of the women behind the workers, and an approach to management that embodies building connection as opposed to role identification, which creates isolation. Hey, is that really her job? Yes. This work is a different animal and I say yes, the responsibility of management is far different than at any other type of workplace.

Women's experience with confrontation and challenge is inextricably linked to power and control, and our perception of their use is often over-whelmingly negative, since it has invited gender stereotypes of non-feminine behaviour and deeply rooted misogynistic consequences. Our socialization has provided us with negative views of power, challenge and confrontation, and these views have become imbedded in our psyche as our own. Some theorize that women's source of power comes from our community, as community is defined in each woman's life (family, workplace, church group), and the risk of confrontation is the danger of being cut off from that community, thus becoming further disempowered. Should the woman use her power, she might precipitate attack and abandonment, cutting to the core of her fear of the loss of connectedness. Given these factors and women's felt sense of historical and societal disempowerment, arriving at the stage where group members can confront each other is a challenge in itself. It requires faith that all will not be lost should a worker put forth a challenge to another. This is an area of personal growth with which many women are not accustomed, and it is one that we as counsellors strive to bring our clients to, yet often shy away from ourselves. As front-line workers we may find the wherewithal to question authority, but we find it extremely difficult to challenge a peer and risk direct expressions of anger and disagreement. More than often, the expressions of these emotions are carried out through non-direct avenues (thus we witness the great phenomenon of passive-aggressive behaviour) and effect no change whatsoever.

So why can we tell a client she must find her voice, challenge in order to change and confront in order to gain empowerment, yet find ourselves unable to do this in our interpersonal relationships within the workplace? This occurs because we refuse to acknowledge our own enormous power over the vulnerable woman we are "helping," and we stumble through with blindfolds and carry out an enormous hypocrisy. If the management of the agency and the individual members have worked to create a climate in which challenge and change can safely unfold, we will learn that conflict and connection can exist simultaneously. And as women, in our experience for the most part, conflict and connection have never co-existed and seem unlikely to co-exist.

> The women's groups that self-destruct today do so because they are structured for consensus; because they encourage a style of speech that places at its centre the question, "What hurts?" rather than, "What can be done?"; because women think they have to like each other personally and work through their differences instead of working with them; and because women are unused to the idea that they can gather to share power and pleasure. Women tend to assume that a group must do some self-sacrificing chore rather than create resources for its own members and open up opportunities for others in a way that feels good. In its new phase, feminism must begin to utilize the only substance strong enough to forge coalitions from the diverse agendas of those who constitute the majority of the human population: mutual self-interest bolstered by impersonal respect. (Wolf 1994: 296)

THE WAYS OF SILENCING

> *The Board told us that they would no longer have any direct communication with staff and would not accept any letters from them. They also denied our request to have a staff rep at board meetings. We were rendered without a voice at all. — C*

Structure is inherent in silencing and maintaining the status quo. If how the concept of the structure is flipped within an agency and the definition of roles is played with to create a more realistic sense of what is required in each role, then the old concept of structure and the power imbalance inherent within it gets flipped on its head. Realistically, the role of managers is to serve front-line staff.

We as women are silenced within our agencies because the structures and unconscious behaviours are still indicative of patriarchy. Even if no man is running the agency, if a woman embraces patriarchal frameworks and cultural norms, the man is ever-present.

The front-line worker has no power, no ability to evaluate the executive director, no avenue to the board, no avenue to give direct feedback without the risk of punishment. There needs to be built-in better evaluation tools to give voice to all staff. As it stands within many organizations, trying to forge a channel of communication with the board or upper management can lead to direct or indirect harassment. My interviewees told me over and over again that criticism and critique can only be heard when staff have a sense of belonging, acceptance and respect. Those who are in positions of structural power are the least willing to engage in mutual feedback.

Unspoken Ways to Silence

Oppression: The sad reality of VAW work and silence is the sad irony is that we are only now really getting around to doing anti-racism and anti-oppression work, and when we were supposed to be about fighting for equality, why was that missed? Why did the women of colour need to be the ones who had to ram it into our brains? Why are women of colour still the ones carrying the load of this agenda?

Victimization: The "who is more victimized" theme is also played out within many agencies and once again speaks to a terrible lack of leadership and lack of adequate support and debriefing. For many who truly need support, none exists. For those who use power disguised as victimization, there seems to be ample room for airing their woes.

The Outcast: Too often those who have spoken out against wrongdoing are scapegoated and cast out. Many women have described being "run out" of an agency or team and cited that, coincidentally, they were the vocal members of the group who pointed out injustices and inconsistencies.

No Room for Questions: Are we ever actually listening to one another? We profess to be listening to the women, but are we even paying attention to each other?

We Never Show Our Own Humanity: To our staff or to each other we are afraid of disclosing our own humanity, our personal selves for fear this exposure may increase our vulnerability. There can be no acknowledgment that we are always working through our own stuff as women and are on a path of healing from something. We all need to be in supportive counselling, or have access to it, to ethically work with others and maintain healthy inner selves. We need to be cognizant of important anniversaries, benchmarks and cycles, and this needs to be spearheaded by supervisors but must be reflected within the greater team. I do not mean making sure everyone signs a card for their birthday. I refer to those deeply personal commemorations that have shaped who we are and how we feel, and thus how we are within the workplace. It may take time and trust before information is shared of such a personal nature, but once it is, it must be respected and accommodated.

The Impostors: The Secret to Everything is just tell them what they want to hear (otherwise known as the False Reality Syndrome). You can be a respected counsellor, peer, get into management, all the while just spitting out rhetoric.

The women who get revered as the "experts" are deemed to be the ones "in the know," and the women who get left out may be equally knowledgeable but have not acquired a personality following.

Can I Actually Be a Lesbian or Is It All Just Rhetoric? Wherever there are women, some of them are lesbian. Many VAW agencies who profess to have an anti-racism/anti-oppression framework have women afraid to disclose they are lesbian. This is at all levels of the structure, including the executive director.

I'm Sorry, But You're Just Too Feminine: You are too feminine, you are wearing makeup, you are married, etc. There are many, many reasons to scapegoat and render a colleague's voice silent rather than celebrating differences.

We fight for social change but loathe change within our agencies. I once saw the filing of a grievance because someone rearranged the position of a desk. Here are some issues with change:

- everyone wants to feel they had input;
- it affects the sense of safety;
- there is a loss of a sense of control over your environment and you are working in a chaotic work environment already;
- we fight so much for positioning within our staff groups that when there is a change, we are painfully aware there will be another shift and we will have to start from square one gaining our position back;
- everything else has already changed for us emotionally and spiritually.

Often, women refuse to own their own issues. Okay girls, we all know this happens. So why do we continue to perpetuate this awful phenomenon when as feminists we should be aware of our behaviour and self-reflecting to ensure we are not acting oppressively? Studies have showed that extremely large numbers of women will be sabotaged on the job by another woman (Heim 2003; Briles 2000). The overall trend toward increasing violence by women has everything to do with adopting the male use of power and the mechanisms adapted by women-led organizations to mainstream male models.

It has nothing to do with biology, chromosomes or hormones. We aren't evil or born to backbite. It's a coping mechanism we are forced to use because power is denied us. — Leora Tanenbaum

---

As I was researching I came across other stories of women who felt ostracized and excluded from the core group, or terminated from an agency, for reasons they felt were due to their beliefs in things like goddesses, or because they practised alternative therapies outside the agency, or drummed, or wore the wrong pants. One group was accused of running a cult and their manager of brainwashing them.

Many stories relayed comments made to them that were accusatory and intolerant. A couple had been called witches directly, or witchcraft was implied. Those whom the mainstream world could not wrap their minds around, those of whom the mainstream was afraid, were branded with the terrible historical label of witch, and subsequently "burned." The burning of course took the form of sanctions, punitive discipline, scapegoating and group ex-communication. Creating our own symbolic witches within the feminist community is terribly significant.

How staff members react to issues, challenges or conflict has everything to do with how they are feeling about the agency as a whole in that moment. This might be a reaction to a chain of events or single event, such as a dismissal of a staff member, or the alteration of a shift schedule or changes to a program, generally all of which were decided and carried out by management or a supervisor, often without the input or knowledge of front-line staff. What occurs then is that staff, even generally benign staff, react to management decisions or internal conflicts in a manner that is much more confrontational, hostile, rigid and unreasonable than they would have at another time.

This can be witnessed in unionized agencies that reflect a high number of grievances, often of a nature that could have been resolved informally, had the organization not been in a crisis state.

What members of what other field struggle with trying to make themselves totally accessible to everyone? Here is one reason why we have such a hard time. Think of a financial group. What do they care if they are accessible to transgendered women? In our theoretical desire to be accessible to all women, we fail to see where we are not. Consider the following:

Women of colour/First Nations women: Why are we not getting it? "Failure to include a clear commitment to an integrated, anti-racist, feminist service delivery system in the foundation documents of your agency suggests that the organization and its governing body do not support this goal" (OAITH 2000: 12).

Clients facing multiple barriers: Ritual abuse/sadistic sexual abuse survivors, homeless women, those with psychiatric issues, sex trade workers. We have too little internal education, too little confrontation on bias, too little introspection. These women have enough to deal with without having to educate us too.

Women who might be too complicated to let in: Transgendered women. Women with boy children. Lesbian women in abusive relationships — who decides who is the abuser?

TRAUMA AND INTROSPECTION

Humiliation and degradation are becoming an alarmingly prevalent new dimension in reported assaults. Women are speaking more freely about their torture, which is healthy, but for the counsellor absorbing the information, this is often too much to bear. There appears to be little internal dialogue about this trend towards increased heinous cruelty or the impact it has on the listener. Once again, we are providing insufficient support for staff in the area of clinical supervision and stress management.

To be in the work of violence against women and in a heterosexual relationship, a woman must deconstruct her own relationship within a feminist framework and in doing so acknowledge core power imbalances and other foundations of an abusive construct. This is not to say that she is abused within the context as we have framed it for the purposes of creating penal codes, family law, education and counselling models, but should we look beyond that safety net. There still is a divisive form of "us and them," and women of conscience must be truthful.

The approach to feminist counselling has incorporated the importance of examining the patriarchal framework and of self-disclosure as it relates to the forward momentum of a woman's counselling experience. However, I have rarely seen a counsellor approach a woman's situation with both the camaraderie of the acknowledgment of heterosexual love and the distance to remain objective. I have witnessed one counsellor, for whom I have enormous respect, do this tremendously. She portrayed the natural evolution of seeing herself within the work and within the world. Too often these highly intuitive counsellors are chastized for using too much self-disclosure, healing themselves or not creating professional distance. I see this woman as constantly trying to create a community of women, not professional distance. This is an art and can be abused by a woman who is seeking solely to help herself.

As a well-meaning young woman in this field, I worked in the children's program, which involved teaching "parenting," of all things, using non-corporal punishment, discipline, etc. I recall the open hostility toward me by one mom. She asked me who I thought I was, telling her anything about parenting, about being a mom, when I had not even had kids. I felt I had the right, since I had a background in this field as a child of a battered woman. I was young, stupid and naïve. When I matured and had children of my own I realized why she must have felt anger. I was no one to tell her how to parent, especially in the face of her abuse. She did what she could, as best as she could.

The set-up of course was the structure of the program, which dictated I offer these services — instructional and teaching services — rather than resource-based, or support-based or peer-based services. We need to ensure that what and how we offer help is not patronizing or demeaning and that it respects women's capacity and journey.

How we respond in the workplace is deeply altered when we already have underlying issues of our own herstory of being a survivor. This experience alters how we accept criticism, how we deal with conflict, how we might unconsciously recreate trauma in our lives, all of which interferes with our ability to work. Our experience changes the nature of client/counsellor dynamics and our sense of safety within the world and the microcosm of our workplace.

As Judith Herman puts it, the survivor's relationships with other people tend to oscillate between extremes as the survivor attempts to establish a sense of safety. The problematic area here is this: if we assume that all staff are wrestling with trauma, then turning to one another can be dangerous territory. Safety must be established by the agency itself; it must create a strong, safe, confidential container.

We have been brainwashed into thinking we must portray ourselves to our clients and each other as devoid of experience of abuse. Or, if we use self-disclosure with our clients, it is viewed as a specific tool to generate response from the woman, and the extent of self-disclosure is carefully monitored. This grossly negates connection between women. It also negates women's ability to filter out, absorb and process information they receive, as if they are mindless fragile sponges who will be damaged if they knew their counsellor hides an abuse history behind her nicely pressed clothes.

> *I did a training one night on ritual abuse for the new volunteers. I am a survivor and disclosed that, not to garner any sympathy, but so these women could realize this does happen, and the survivors are not freaks. Well, another staff present reported me to the board of directors, said I had no boundaries and was inappropriate. — R*

The Creation of Good and Bad Clients

Another issue that polarizes staff is in how we perceive the client herself. The values and norms of the individual staff member, regardless of her ethical responsibility to be unbiased, do interfere with direct service delivery. Issues of race, class, cognitive ability, mental health, street women, sex trade workers and drug users are the more common presenting hurdles for acceptance. Often these women are judged and stereotyped upon admission, and the counsellors who demonstrate this intolerance are rarely challenged by their peers. Commonly, these women face a double bias: one from the staff, and the other from other residents, who may band together and align themselves against the "different" woman. Women who are already marginalized entering the shelter system may be further marginalized within the safety of the shelter, with the bias of the staff and residents now transforming itself into a more insidious oppression within the guise of unfounded accusations against the woman, i.e., theft, aggression, sexual harassment.

The real shame in many of these instances is the inability of the counselling staff to tackle these issues with directness and capability. Now the problem of the staff's own bias will often feed into the scapegoating of this woman because of her response to the complaints of other residents and the lack of open dialogue within the larger group (i.e., emergency house meetings, which I have seen counsellors avoid or refuse to facilitate). Too often, counselling staff will "side" with clients who are easy to manage, less disruptive, the good girls, and begin to frame the "bad" woman now as a threat to the women within the shelter, a bad mix, a risk.

I have seen counsellors with years of experience in shelters refuse to work with a woman, citing that they did not feel safe. One went so far as to lock herself in the counselling office for her entire shift and wore her panic button if she was forced to leave her sanctuary. This message was quickly picked up by the other residents (not to mention the client herself), who were already beginning to gel as a group against the woman they viewed as hostile. The counsellor was quick to receive the complaints from the other residents, but did not address the issues directly with anyone and avoided dealing with concrete inappropriate actions this woman had demonstrated. Instead, the fear blossomed, and eventually this client was asked to leave, with staff feeling it necessary to have police stand by.

This was a street woman, gruff, foul-mouthed and lesbian. She had many real violence and safety issues and was ready and willing to deal with them, but found herself in a very middle-class homophobic institution. There were glaring examples of homophobia having played a huge role in the reactions of the staff, but no one was willing to engage in dialogue about this possibility after the fact, nor own any responsibility or accountability for homophobic behaviour.

> *I was doing her admit forms. We got to the question of what she did for a living. I asked her, so what do you do? She said, "I'm a dancer." She was trying to be polite to me, trying to make me comfortable, worried about what I thought about her and her choice of profession as a stripper. Of course, this was all way over my head, and I assumed in my classist world of privilege. I said to her, "oh, ballet?"* — C

I was working at a rape crisis centre and a new strip club was opening up in our community. We took a strong stand as a group, fought it in council, utilized the media, tried to educate the public about the correlation of exploitation and abuse. In the end, the club opened, albeit with very tough by-laws and unhappy owners, but we received a response from a woman who was a stripper. She challenged us that we had never been representing her. She worked in a field that was riddled with abuses of working women, and in our intolerance and the moral righteousness of our anti-strip-club stand, we had totally closed the doors to the women who worked there, some of whom may have badly needed our services.

It is essential to work through our biases as we make agency decisions. Too often we are not even exploring them. They might not be manifesting in clear-cut racist or homophobic ways (although too many agencies have been openly homophobic), but might be transforming how we work with women in ways that are not helpful to them. For example, we might not confront women clients on their racist remarks or explain consequences for breaching rules well enough, which leads to women being kicked out of residential shelters.

We must have more opportunities for self-discovery within a team-building context. We must permit ourselves a safe environment to explore and challenge ourselves and our messages and the beliefs programmed into us since birth.

Building Community

All women have the potential to be abused. This is not an "illness" that requires treatment but a circumstance that happens to women. Abuse creates great isolation and that isolation helps to keep women in abusive situations. Remediation then is in helping women to live in community, to build trusting relationships with women that support them. This kind of community makes it easier for women to leave or refuse abusive relationships with men. This is tough, just as it is tough to build working relationships with other women in women's organizations. Learning relationship-building to create loving communities is the work of healing. However, a counselling relationship, however skilfully done, replicates a "power over" relationship. In the drive to create feminist therapy in the early 1990s, many women's services lost the capacity to create community in the rush to professionalize their services.

Many women say they stay in this work like an abusive relationship, hoping it'll get better. The simple answer is not, "If it's that bad, go get another job." Giving up on women's organizational structures that offer anti-violence services would be like writing off your own mother. Anti-violence work bleeds its way into every part of your life. Once you have the framework and this enlightened reality, it is impossible to turn a blind eye to the oppression and abuses in the "real world." It is impossible not to analyze, not to challenge, not to feel anger.

Building communities of women and connections between women is an integral key to equalization of power. Yet I see feminist communities transforming themselves into exclusive communities and putting each other down with quiet subversion, undermining those outside of the community, devaluing their work, belittling their value. The community is then perceived as all-knowing, as the agent of truth, and the power bestowed to them excludes those who might otherwise have a voice, or at the very least, wish to be heard.

You do not want the others to turn on you, so you create ways to keep the spotlight off yourself and maybe hint at on whom the spotlight should be, before they turn and devour you.

> There is a very hidden aspect to most collectives that encourages oppression of women's wild, soulful, and creative lives, and that is the encouragement within the culture for women themselves to "tell on" one another and to sacrifice their sisters to strictures that do not reflect the relatedness found in the familial values of the feminine nature. These include not only the encouraging of one woman to inform on another and therefore expose her to punishment for behaving in a feminine and integral manner, for registering appropriate horror or dissension to injustice, but also the encouraging of older women to collude in the physical, mental, and spiritual abuse of women who are younger, less powerful, or helpless, and the encouraging of young women to dismiss and neglect the needs of women who are far older than they. (Estes 1995: 241)

> And so at times we perform little clitoridectomy equivalents on ourselves. We reject the idea of sisterhood and of female solidarity. We make fun of it. We scorn the term feminist, roll our eyes at it. We say we're beyond it, we're all fine... we have so much aggression in us, we're so alive, we're wild, golden-eyed, and strong, and we take out our pistols and shoot at each other, or at the floor, at our glass-slippered feet. (Angier 2000: 283)

Are we creating the false sense of shelter anonymity out of shame or confidentiality? Are we using the notion of client confidentiality falsely? Why can't we be friends with clients? Who are the boundaries we have created really for? Are they because we cannot accept the continuum of healing and change?

Are We Really Afraid of Our Clients?

I witnessed this fear of clients being manifested in several ways. Administration is often structured to be as far as possible from the residents' physical space. One administration built itself the equivalent of an "ivory tower" next to the shelter. There was security between the buildings on the inside and the admin staff never went into the shelter. They had separate everything. The staff administrators had newspaper delivery and a cleaner for themselves, which were not offered to the women in the shelter. It is as if we have fear by association of the abused women, as if their issues may rub off onto our lives. What is the structure of counselling offices? How are the desks placed? Is your back to the door? Do the counsellors join women for meals or eat alone in the office?

It seems to be a survival mechanism, in which if we can keep ourselves removed even by one degree, physically, by title, by function, we can separate ourselves from "those women" and remain elitist, one step above them. We fear that women clients could easily be us. Is this why the shelter movement needed to professionalize? Apart from the argument that we were seeking respect from other so called "professionals" in court and other bureaucratic playing fields, did we need to shield ourselves from our common experience? Violence and pain are the reality of the experience clients bring through the door. But I have seen counsellors go to the trouble of Creative Logging: Sorry, no time to see the woman. By word-smithing in our notes we can choose whom we service.

So many women clients want to give back and those of us in paid positions are often reluctant to give way to women volunteering "too soon." Who can determine when is too soon for someone else? Is the fear really that she will take our job; will attack; cannot be fixed, will not be accountable; is not trained. What constitutes training? We are fighting the BSW, but then we use it against the volunteering women. Why do we fear the creation of community? Residential service is only one small compartment of serving abused women. We have underestimated and misread the real needs of women.

Women in the Field: Why Are We Here?

It makes me wonder sometimes, really wonder, how when yet another woman is murdered we can stomach going into work and safety-planning with other women. It certainly is not for the money. As Michele Landsberg, columnist for the *Toronto Star,* put it:

> The worst moocher in the provincial government is the provincial government itself. For six years the government has been shamelessly sponging off the backbreaking work of women whose job it is to prevent domestic murder. You would think that those who help make society stronger, safer and less violent would be at least rewarded for their labours.

She went on to expose the shameful cuts in funding in the Province of Ontario to violence-against-women services and says:

Nevertheless, the workers in that high stress field did not slacken their efforts or chintz on service. They stretched themselves thinner and thinner, and used precious hours of leisure time to beg for charity and write up grant proposals. (Landsberg 2002)

However, many such staff were quick to point out colleagues they felt were too issue-driven to be honest with themselves in this work and therefore harmful, with or without conscious intention, to the women they are serving. They fit into the following categories:

The Saint — These are those who pretend they have no bias, no racist bone in their body. The ultimate barrier for white women to true anti-racism work is to pretend we are totally politically correct.

The Martyr — Those who do good things so others will notice create dependency. Martyrs arise when members of a miserable group turn their repressions inwards and evolve into a "hierarchy of miserable saintliness. Members competed for the most exhausting tasks, the most stressful time slots on the phone." (Wolf 1994: 157)

Women who Need to Be Clients, Not Staff — We sometimes expect from our workplace and co-workers what we do not get from our families, or we expect them to behave in the same ways. We replicate our roles with everyone: mothers, sisters, lovers. Becoming aware of ourselves and feminism are not mutually exclusive. We grow into a violence-against-women worker. It is a lifelong journey of learning and growth. As we remain in this field, so too must we constantly take stock of the health of our own lives.

Creating Safety

In order to accept the need for creation of safety in the workplace environment of shelters and sexual assault centres, we must accept the premise that all women have been traumatized, are part of a collective unconscious of oppression and pain, and have as individuals perhaps been directly affected by abuse. We must accept that as organizations, agencies and a business identity we have also been traumatized by the manner in which our agencies have been run, how we as staff have been treated, how we are perceived by other mainstream services, the undermining of our mandates by funders and the overriding attitudes in society.

As construction workers of feminist agencies we must be cognizant of and also beware of symbolism: the accidental recreation of traumatic frameworks or environments. If we operate from the premise that women embody the unconscious trauma of oppression, regardless of specific experience or "degree" of victimization, then the central task in creating a healthy organization is establishing safety. If we look at this within the context of therapeutic healing, safety is the central task of the first stage of recovery.

Judith Herman, author of the definitive work on trauma and recovery, who synthesized the experiences of combat veterans, victims of political terror and survivors of rape and domestic violence, examines the recovery process. She lays out three stages of recovery: the first being the establishment of safety, the second stage being mourning and remembrance and the third stage reconnection with ordinary life. She lays these out as abstract concepts, to attempt to impose a simplicity on a complex process, and in that construct, acknowledges that no recovery follows a linear course: "Oscillating and dialectical in nature, the traumatic syndromes defy any attempt to impose such simpleminded order. In fact, patients and therapists alike frequently become discouraged when issues that have supposedly been put to rest stubbornly reappear" (Herman 1992: 155). Another therapist has described the progression through the stages of recovery as a spiral, in which earlier issues are continually revisited on a higher level of integration. If the premise exists that all women embody collective unconscious trauma, and the truth of the matter is that most women in their lifetime will experience direct violent acts, and if the truth of the career path of women who enter violence-against-women work is a homecoming to what they inherently understand through personal experience, then all staff at every hierarchical level within violence against women agencies have the potential for their trauma to reappear and to oscillate between stages of recovery throughout the duration of employment, despite their level of healing upon hire.

It is paramount then to create an atmosphere of safety in which women can work. It is not enough that women house their personal experiences and embodiment of trauma, but the nature of the work, the vicarious trauma and the secondary trauma of their connection with clients, further adds to the material that must be massaged into recovery.

Despite all the research, few agencies actually name the trauma as such. There is little acknowledgement of the experience of trauma of front-line workers in a secondary victimization context. There are few opportunities built into the regular work schedule for psychological de-briefing, personal or professional. There exists a very male attitude toward feeling and emotional residue from the work, in that the staff are not expected to be affected by their work And the clear expectation is that staff be entirely "healed" and free and clear of any leftovers from their experiences with violence, although there is little or no dialogue concerning these issues within the job interview or subsequent employment supervision.

This is not to say that women who are in a state of crisis of spirit should be in the position of helping when they themselves require more support than would their client. That would be unethical in that their issues and emotional needs may spill out into the client relationship, thus placing the client in the role of counsellor, doing that woman a disservice in not allowing her to access the assistance she requires. Where we trip all over ourselves is in acknowledging that crisis runs a river through women's lives, widening and narrowing at life intervals, and somehow we manage to keep the rest of our lives together, carry on and continue to grow and heal. The injustice lies in the fact that staff are forced into the terrible position of having to hide any trauma like a dirty little secret. It is a hideous recreation of an abusive relationship, placing the agency and those who manage it in the role of the abuser.

If the workplace is open about the reality of trauma and can create an environment of safety, then individuals who are at stages of their spiralling healing can be afforded the chance to request help for themselves, to practice self-care, and the manager can then feel comfortable in asking if the staff does indeed require assistance, if they might be struggling at the moment; this inquiry would be received well, given the intention behind it. Being permitted the chance to name the issue and to have a plan set up for how to assist would dramatically decrease burnout, spiritual exhaustion and residual effects of the self-denial of pain. Judith Herman cites the role of the therapist to reframe accepting help as an act of courage and maintains that acknowledging the reality of one's condition and taking the steps to change it are signs of strength, not weakness, initiative, not passivity. Certainly this must be the role of the manager or executive director as well.

But many staff are well founded in their fear and reluctance to "disclose" in the workplace. One reason is that we have managed to bastardize the concept of boundaries to mean being devoid of feeling and experience. One shelter I know of demanded psychological testing, with the results given to the executive director. Shelter staff have witnessed colleagues being disciplined, terminated and scapegoated for disclosing too much of their personal selves.

Management's primary response is more than often this: it is not my role to act as therapist. This is a job, a place of business; if you need help go and get it on your own, you are a grown woman. I do support ensuring that all staff have a strong support system external to the agency. This can be anybody, from paid therapist to close friend, but the support must be external. Having external supports creates a necessary distance from the work environment, creating clarity, balance. But this must not absolve the agency from responsibility to provide staff with internal supports.

Is it part of the role of managers to work in a therapeutic capacity? If trauma robs the victim of a sense of power and control, the guiding principle of recovery is to restore power and control to the survivor (Herman 1992: 159). Is it not imbedded in the mandate of anti-violence agencies to address the imbalance of power and control as it exists within patriarchal structures and to empower women in addressing such injustices? It must be an internal function to assist female staff in restoring their sense of power and control in a refocused, healthy manner through many avenues, including the establishment of safety and healing from trauma, social action and political activism.

Herman states that survivors feel unsafe in their bodies. Establishing control must begin with control over the body and move gradually outward toward control over the environment. Issues of bodily integrity include attention to "basic health needs, regulation of bodily functions such as sleep, eating and exercise, management of post traumatic symptoms, and control of self destructive behaviours. Environmental issues include establishment of a safe living situation and financial security" (Herman 1992: 160).

Basic Health Needs

Sleep: Shelter workers, most of whom work shifts, are faced with schedules that fluctuate between day, evening and overnight work. Staff are often poorly scheduled as a direct result of underfunding and meagre numbers of full-time staff to cover shifts. Virtually no one in my front-line group of informants could say they had a healthy sleeping pattern. The only regularity seemed to exist in the standard norm of sleep deprivation. Shift work in and of itself has been studied at length, primarily on male subjects, and has been found to be extremely unhealthy, both physically and emotionally (see, for example, Statistics Canada 2002; Freudenberger 1983; Circadian Technologies 2003). I am certain that in an equivalent study, women would fare far worse as we do not have a "caretaker" in the home attempting to provide balance for the shift worker as most of the male test subjects had. It is the exception, not the norm, for a shelter or sexual assault worker not to be the sole or primary caregiver in a given family.

Eating: Regulation of eating habits for those who work, especially in the residential shelter settings, is virtually impossible. Shift work is not conducive to healthy eating habits, nor are residential care environments. Snacking is the norm, and front-line workers rely on grazing to get them through a shift that often leaves no time to actually sit and eat with the women. Cultural differences in cooking may also play a factor, as does vegetarianism, two sorely overlooked accommodations of both staff and residents.

Another disturbing fact is just how many women in this field have admitted to having an eating disorder. We are a product of the Barbie world, and a devastatingly high number of women who should "know better" are still starving, purging, using other dangerous weight-loss practices and just as entangled in the residual garbage of a beauty archetype we should be completely divorced from.

Exercise: Regular exercise is a hurdle for many front-line crisis counsellors. This is a result of shift work or a lack of financial resources to join a gym in which it is comfortable to work out. Primarily though, this lack of attention to the physical form manifests in the embodiment of trauma and unmassaged pain, and also the seeming juxtaposition of anti-violence work and the caretaking of a healthy female body. There is much overlapping here, socialized issues we can wade in knee-deep that are about the body of a woman and "preoccupation" with its appearance.

Control of Self-Destructive Behaviours: Little attention is paid to preventative measures for staff such as effective self-care: self-care that is self-determined and supported. Attention is only paid when the fallout begins, when burnout is active, spreading through the agency, manifesting as sick time, internal sabotage or indirect aggression. The cure then turns again to mainstream solutions: discipline and termination — never healing strategies or the seeking of an agency-wide cure.

Establishment of Safe Living and Financial Security: Providing staff with the financial ability to lead a good life and have choices goes a long way in promoting the health of employees and organizations. Options range from wages, to benefit plans, to pensions, to providing staff with opportunities to seek advice from financial advisors, to alternative therapies.

Self Punishment while Working with Victims: The woman with privilege by virtue of her position on the other side of the desk, the one not in immediate victimization, the one with the job, can be tempted to fall into unconscious self-punishment. Once again, healing rituals, healing circles and agency-sanctioned retreats are ways to combat this.

Support Systems: If staff members do not have an individual external support system, the agency must provide them with an internal one.

Self-Care Practice: "To name your work 'political,' especially when it comes to your body and to things that are 'womanly' is an act of power.... If you're healing a fibroid tumour or remembering your incest, you are doing political work" (Northrup 1994: 12).

Recognize When It Is Time to Take a Break from the Work: Workers use anti-depressants to carry on in the work when what is really needed is either a break from the work or adequate internal supports that offer debriefing or healing.

Substance Use/Abuse:

> Systematic stuffing or denying of our needs for self-expression and self-actualization causes us enormous emotional pain. To stay out of touch with our pain, women have commonly used addictive substances and developed addictive behaviors that have resulted in an endless cycle of abuse that we ourselves help perpetuate. Being abused or abusing ourselves, we become ill. When we become ill, we are treated by a patriarchal medical system that denigrates our bodies. (Northrup 1994: 13)

So states Christiane Northrup in *Women's Bodies, Women's Wisdom,* who draws the correlation between patriarchy and addiction and holds that this connection is the key to understanding women's major health problems.

Solutions

- A breakfast club: How much would it really cost the agency to have fresh fruit for staff when they arrive?
- Pick your battles before they manifest in your body: There are often too many battles to fight in this field by virtue of the work itself, the community, the structures, the internal politics, etc. Our bodies cannot withstand this onslaught; we need to spend time in reflection to sort out which battles need to be fought and which ones can be carried by others, or by the agency, or which need to be dumped therapeutically.
- Getting a sense of humour/sneaking joy: This is not to say that violence is fun, but anti-violence work can be fun, and camaraderie in sisterhood should definitely be fun.
- Celebrating victories: Even small ones.

THE ISSUES THAT THREATEN TO DEPLETE US

We delude ourselves into believing that women are always forthright and that a small faction of women with other multiple needs are not pulling our legs. If we acknowledge that women sometimes lie and abuse the system, and demonstrate a consistent assessment that *allows* for these anomalies, then we will not feel foolish or out of line if such situations come to light. The problem is that in our society, the woman-blaming theme is so common and the political climate so eager to pull funds, we are too afraid to tackle this problem. We need to train ourselves to educate and be spokeswomen to offset destructive arguments.

"Don't women abuse too?" This is the oldest tactic used to silence what we know to be truth. Too often we engage in this futile rhetoric. We are wasting energy. First and foremost, protect your issue. Such inflammatory comments are Trojan horses. Do not allow them.

The frustration that women are still being murdered weighs heavily on our shoulders. We find ourselves in a place of spiritual meltdown, blaming ourselves for being ineffectual, not changing the course of femicide. Yet we rarely talk about this terrible feeling as a group within our agencies, and when our clients are murdered, agency response is varied (perhaps lacking in critical incident planning) and often woefully inadequate. As workers, we feel as though all we do does not matter, really — not the counselling, the groups or the public talks. This is a dangerous abyss, into which all staff will fall sooner or later; or the entire agency will collectively tumble in when one of its own is murdered. Remember the following:

- We are fulfilling our role as we have defined it and therefore cannot bear responsibility for the lack of societal change.
- No one else is picking up the ball to stop the violence.
- If we feel ineffective, maybe we are. Maybe we need to restructure to create and direct opportunity for social action.

As consumers of mainstream media we are subjected to the sensationalism of rape and violence rather than the reality of the systemic and persistent abuse that is the world of our clients and ourselves. There have been few actual shifts in public perceptions of violence against women, and the prevalence of these crimes in our media shows a lack of education or morals.

> There is now a dangerous schism between rhetoric and reality in discussions of sexual violence. While there is now a symbolic acceptance for the concept of sexual assault as both a "crime" and an unacceptable violation, the number of assaults that are viewed and treated as legitimate has in fact declined. These days, only a very small proportion of survivors are afforded the credibility and social support they deserve. (Khosla 2003: 18)

Women's growing use or acceptance of pornography and its insidious creep into mainstream is not a reclamation of an oppressive tool, like reclaiming language. We need to be informed consumers.

This is imperative that we have a national women's movement. We must give women a voice on the national stage, the world stage. Our voice is lost, splintered and divided. We need to seek commonalities, no matter what they might be, to join women with other women and begin to carve out a national identity, national platforms and a strong unified voice.

- Matrons need to fund it.

- Women need to support other women seeking political careers.
- Women need to be party-blind.
- Women need to infiltrate the media and impregnate the social, cultural conscious.
- Women need common symbols.

SELECT BIBLIOGRAPHY

Angier, Nathalie. 2000. *Woman: An Intimate Geography.* New York: Anchor.

Belenky, Mary, Blythe Clinchy, Nancy Goldberger and Jill Tarule. 1997. *Women's Ways of Knowing: The Development of Self, Voice, and Mind.* New York: Harper Collins.

Bishop, Anne. 2002. *Becoming An Ally: Breaking the Cycle of Oppression in People.* Halifax: Fernwood Publishing.

Bountrogianni, Dr. Marie M.P.P. 2002. *End of Term Report.* Toronto

Briles, Judith. 1999. *Woman to Woman 2000: Becoming Sabotage Savvy in the New Millennium.* New Horizon Press.

Brown, C., and K.M. O'Brien. 1998. "Understanding Stress and Burnout in Shelter Workers." *Professional Psychology: Research and Practice* 29, 4: 383–85.

Brown, Laura. 1991. "Antiracism as an Ethical Imperative: An Example from Feminist Therapy." *Ethics and Behaviour* 1(2), 113–27.

Bula, Judith. 1999. "Differential Use of Self by Therapists Following their Own Trauma Experiences." In Michele Baldwin (ed.), *The Use of Self in Therapy.* New York: Columbia University Press.

Butler, Sandra, and Claire Wintram. 1991. *Feminist Groupwork.* London: Sage Publications.

Circadian Technologies, Inc. 2003 *Healthy Study Release.* Circadian Technologies, Inc., MS.

Coroners Report into the Death of Arlene May. 2002. Office of the Chief Coroner, Ontario Domestic Violence Death Review Committee, Annual Report: Case Review of Domestic Violence Deaths.

Delongis, A., S. Folkman, and R. Lazarus. 1998. "The Impact of Daily Stress on Health and Mood: Psychological and Social Resources as Mediators." *Journal of Personality and Social Psychology* 54, 486–95.

Duvall, Jim. 2004. "Focus on Results" (lecture notes). Results Management Training Program, Coaching Series Two, Hinks-Dellcrest Centre, Toronto.

Duxbury, Dr. Linda. 2004. "Creating A Healthy Workplace" (lecture notes). School of Business, Carleton University, Owen Sound.

Estes, Clarissa Pinkola. *Women Who Run with the Wolves.* 1995. New York: Ballantine Books.

Fallding, Helen. 2003. "Why Do Lesbians Batter?" *Herizons* (Spring). Winnipeg, MB

Finn, Janet L. 1990. "Burnout in the Human Services: A Feminist Perspective." *Women and Social Work* 5(4) (Winter), 55–71.

Freire, Paulo. 1997. *Pedagogy of the Oppressed.* New York: Continuum.

Freudenberger, H. 1983. "Burnout: Contemporary Issues, Trends and Concerns." In Farber, (ed.), *Stress and Burnout in the Human Services Professions.* New York:

Pergamon.

Goldberger, Nancy, Jill Tarule, Blythe Clinchy, Mary Belenky (eds.). 1998. *Knowledge, Difference and Power: Essays Inspired by Women's Ways of Knowing*. New York: Basic Books.

Heim, Paticia 2003. *In the Company of Women: Indirect Aggression Among Women, Why We Hurt Each Other and How to Stop*. New York: Putnam.

Herizons. 2003. (Summer). Winnipeg, MB.

Herman, Judith. *Trauma and Recovery*. 1992. New York: Harper Collins.

Jay, Suzanne. 2002. "Asian Women Stand Together to Speak Out Against Violence." *Herizons* (Spring) Winnipeg, MB.

Jordan, Judith V., Alexandra G. Kaplan, Jean Bake Miller, Irene P. Stiver and Janet L. Surrey. 1991. *Women's Growth in Connection*. New York: Guilford Press.

Khosla, Punam. 2003. *Strategic Plan 2003 to 2008*. Toronto: Ontario Coalition of Rape Crisis Centres.

Kurland, Rosella, and Robert Salmon (eds.). 1995. *Group Work Practice In a Troubled Society*. New York: Haworth Press.

Landsberg, Michele. 2002. (column) *Toronto Star*, March 10.

Leoff, Constance. 1987. *Bluff Your Way in Feminism*. London: Ravette.

Lerner, Gerda. 1986. *The Creation of Patriarchy*. New York: Oxford University Press.

Lerner, Harriet. 2004. *The Dance of Deception*. New York: Harper Collins.

Longstreth, George MD. 1998. "Relation Between Physical or Sexual Abuse and Functional Gastrointestinal Disorders." The Permanente Journal 2, 2 (Spring).

Miller, Grant D. et al. 1987. *Implications of the Wounded-Healer Paradigm for the Use of Self in Therapy*. Binghampton, New York: Haworth Press.

Miller, Jean Baker. 1991. *Women and Power*. New York: Guilford Publications.

Mitchell, J.T., and A. Dyregrov. 1996. "Traumatic Stress in Disaster Workers and Emergency Personnel." *International Handbook of Traumatic Stress Syndromes*. Plenum Press.

Myerhoff, B. 1982. *A Crack in the Mirror: Reflective Perspectives in Anthropology*. Philadelphia: University of Pennsylvania Press.

Northrup, Christiane. 1994. *Women's Bodies, Women's Wisdom*. New York: Bantam Books.

Notzel, Helen. 2004. "Team Coaching: Moving From Management to Leadership" (lecture notes). Hinks-Dellcrest Centre, Toronto.

Ontario Association of Interval and Transition Houses, Anti-Racism/Anti-Oppression Committee. 2000. *Creating Inclusive Spaces for Women*. Toronto.

Ontario Auditor's Report. 2001. Toronto.

Pearson, Patricia. 1997. *When She Was Bad*. New York: Viking Press.

Richardson, Jan. 1991. *Guidebook on Vicarious Trauma: Recommended Solutions for Anti-Violence Workers*. Ottawa: National Clearinghouse on Family Violence, Government of Canada.

Robinson, Laura. 2002. *Black Tights*. Toronto: Harper Collins.

Rosella Kurland and Robert Salmon (eds.), *Groupwork Practice in a Troubled Society*. Haworth Press.

Schachter et al. 2004. "Women Survivors of Child Sexual Abuse." *Canadian Family Physician* March.

Schiller, Linda. 1995. "Stages of Development in Women's Groups: A Relational Model. In Richardson, J. 2001. "Guidebook on Vicarious Trauma: Recommended Solutions for Anti-Violence Workers." National Clearinghouse on Family Violence. Government of Canada.

Sgroi, S. 1988. *Vulnerable Populations.* New York: Simon and Schuster.

Sheldrake. 1994. "The Presence of the Past." In C. Northrup, *Women's Bodies, Women's Wisdom.* New York: Bantam Books.

Statistics Canada. 2002. "Shift Work & Health." *Health Reports* 13, 4 (July). Statistics Canada.

Tenenbaum, Leora. 2003. *Catfight: Rivalries Among Women — from Diets to Dating, from the Boardroom to the Delivery Room.* New York: Harper Collins.

Vermond, Kira. 2004. "The Top Family Friendly Employers in Canada." *Today's Parent* (December/January).

Walsch, N.D. 2002. *Conversations with God*, Book 1. New York: Putnam.

Wolf, Naomi. 1994. *Fire With Fire.* New York: Vintage Canada.